C000214340

*Law*Basics

CONTRACT LAW

SECOND EDITION

AUSTRALIA
Law Book Co.
Sydney

CANADA and USA
Carswell
Toronto

HONG KONG
Sweet & Maxwell Asia

NEW ZEALAND
Brookers
Wellington

SINGAPORE and MALAYSIA
Sweet & Maxwell Asia
Singapore and Kuala Lumpur

*Law*Basics

CONTRACT LAW

SECOND EDITION

By

Alasdair Bothwell Gordon, LL.B., B.D., L.C.G.I., T.Q.F.E.

Formerly Lecturer in Law, Aberdeen College

THOMSON

W. GREEN

Published in 2003 by

W. Green & Son Ltd
21 Alva Street
Edinburgh EH2 4PS

www.wgreen.co.uk

Printed in Great Britain by Athenaeum Press Ltd,
Gateshead, Tyne & Wear

No natural forests were destroyed to make this product;
Only farmed timber was used and replanted

A CIP catalogue record for this book is available from the British Library

ISBN 0 414 01512 6

© W. Green & Son Ltd 2003

All rights reserved. United Kingdom statutory material in this publication
is acknowledged as Crown copyright.

No part of this publication may be reproduced or transmitted in any form
or by any means, or stored in any retrieval system of any nature without
prior written permission, except for permitted fair dealing under the
Copyright, Designs and Patents Act 1988, or in accordance with the terms
of a licence issued by the Copyright Licensing Agency in respect of
photocopying and/or reprographic reproduction. Application for
permission for other use of copyright material including permission to
reproduce extracts in other published works shall be made to the
publishers. Full acknowledgment of author, publisher and source must be
given.

This edition is affectionately dedicated to my mother,
Gena Gordon, who died in January 2003.
A.B.G.

CONTENTS

CONTENTS

TABLE OF CASES

1. THE FORMATION OF CONTRACT

INTRODUCTION

This is the second edition of a modest book on the law of contract in Scotland. It is written by a retired college lecturer to assist students to gain a foundation knowledge of the subject or to use as a revision aid. It is not intended as a substitute for the more scholarly and detailed texts available. Due to constraints of size, a book of this nature cannot go into detailed discussion of issues and the author has restricted himself to a conventional approach. There is a huge body of case law and an attempt has been made to include a reasonable selection of both old and new. Proposals from the Scottish Law Commission for law reform have not been covered in detail, due to constraints of space.

Contract law is, in many ways, the grammar of the whole legal system. Once the basics of this subject have been mastered, the average student will move on to other areas with greater confidence and insight. Purely in the interests of word economy, the book uses masculine terminology but the intention is to be inclusive. Accordingly, "he" means "he or she" and "his" includes "his or her" unless the context clearly indicates otherwise.

It is easy to overlook the fact that contracts feature in many areas of every day life, almost as a matter of course. Many people buy a daily paper and travel by bus to work, but few of them think of these simple transactions as contracts; yet that is precisely what they are. It may be psychologically easier to think in terms of contracts when considering obligations covering items of greater value, such as buying a house or a car. At the risk of over-simplification, the basics of all contracts are the same, whether the subject matter is of high or low value.

The everyday world of business has for centuries been rooted and grounded in the whole concept of a contract being a binding obligation which can be enforced by the parties to it. Most contracts are not expressed in writing. There are some cases where writing is essential and these are explained in Chapter 2. There are certainly cases where writing is desirable, even if not essential, so that the respective rights and duties of the parties are clearly expressed. However, most of the countless number of contracts made every day are purely verbal.

The law of contract, both in Scotland and in England, developed greatly throughout the eighteenth and nineteenth centuries. Many, although by no means all, of the classic cases on contract law date from the nineteenth century. North of the border, contract law is still largely based on common law, with its own distinct Scottish identity and tradition of deducing the law from basic general principles. Whilst there have been major statutory inroads in certain areas, such as under the Sale of Goods

1

Act 1979 and the Consumer Credit Act 1974, the basic law of contract has mainly been developed by the Scottish courts rather than Parliament. In today's more complex society, the trend has been towards a higher degree of statutory or regulatory control. In the 1990s, the Scottish Law Commission presented five significant reports on various aspects of contract law which it saw as being in need of reform. In that decade, the recommendations from only one of these reports passed into legislation in the shape of the Contract (Scotland) Act 1997 (explained in Chapter 8). This raises at least the likelihood of further reforming legislation early in the present century, particularly as there is now a Scottish Parliament.

Also, although they are not binding precedents, it is fair comment to say that many English cases are regarded at least as highly persuasive in Scotland. Under s.126 of the Scotland Act 1998, the law of contract is clearly defined as part of the Scots law of obligations over which the Scottish Parliament has legislative jurisdiction. European Community law also, inevitably, has a growing significance.

WHAT IS A CONTRACT?

A much quoted definition of a contract is that it is "an agreement which creates, or is intended to create, a legal obligation between the parties to it". (Jenks, *Digest of English Civil Law*, 2.1.)

A contract has basically three essential elements: (1) agreement about the same thing, (2) at least two contracting parties and (3) "legal" obligations. Unless all three elements are present, the agreement is not a legally enforceable contract. It may—or may not—be a moral obligation. If it is the latter, the writer of this book is not suggesting that moral obligations should be undertaken or broken lightly. However, the purpose of the book is to concentrate on questions of law and not on moral philosophy. The three elements which make up a contract will now be examined in turn.

Agreement about the same thing

In the traditional textbooks, this concept appears under the maxim *consensus in idem* (agreement about the same thing) and it lies at the very heart of contract law. If there is no real agreement—or the apparent agreement is really about different things—there is no contract. Party A may have two cars, car 1 and car 2. One of them, car 1, is for sale. If party B makes party A an offer for car 2, thinking that is the car for sale—and A accepts the offer, believing that B is actually offering for car 1—both parties think they have a contract. In fact, there is no contract, since there is no agreement on the same thing. In other words the essential *consensus in idem* ("consensus" for short) is lacking. In *Raffles v Wichelhaus* (1864), a cargo was being transported on a ship called *Peerless* from Bombay to England. Unknown to both parties at the time the contract was formed, there were two ships of the same name in Bombay harbour, one sailing in October, the other in December. One party had meant the October ship, the other had intended the ship sailing in December. It was held that there was no consensus and thus no contract. In *Mathieson Gee (Ayrshire) Ltd v Quigley* (1952), a firm of plant hirers offered to hire out plant to remove silt from a pond. The owner of the pond thought that it was an offer to remove the silt, not merely to hire out the plant to do so. As there was no consensus there was no contract.

At least two contracting parties
It is a basic rule of law (and common sense) that it is impossible to have a contract between less than two parties. There is no upper limit, unless created by statute, *e.g.* under the Companies Act 1985, s.716, it is not possible for more than 20 people to enter into a partnership agreement (subject to certain important exceptions). In *Church of Scotland Endowment Committee v Provident Association of London Ltd* (1914), S entered into a purported contract of ground annual with himself. Not surprisingly the "contract" was held to be inept and void.

All parties to the contract must also have the necessary capacity, *i.e.* legal capability, of entering into a contract. This is considered in Chapter 3.

"Legal" obligations
The agreement must create obligations which the law will recognise as being appropriate to enforce, should the need arise. Not surprisingly, the courts will not enforce agreements which are clearly illegal, criminal or immoral. In spite of the catch phrase from the criminal underworld to "put a contract out" on someone (*i.e.* plan an assassination), such an agreement would clearly be illegal and would not be enforced by a court of law. In Chapter 6, consideration is given to contracts which are deemed to be "contractually illegal" because they are contrary to public policy, but not usually thought of as immoral.

However, there are other agreements which are perfectly legal, but which the courts will not uphold. A so-called "social contract", such as a dinner date, is perfectly legal and moral—but if one party fails to turn up, the disappointed party will not be able to compel performance or seek damages.

Social workers, counsellors and others whose role it is to provide personal or emotional support increasingly make "contracts" with their clients. These agreements are frequently in writing. They are intended to be moral, not legal, obligations so that the parties are clear as to boundaries and expectations on both sides.

Also, the court will not enforce betting and gaming wagers, called *sponsiones ludicrae* (obligations in jest) or sportive promises. These agreements, normally, are not illegal but the court will not take any steps to enforce them. In *Kelly v Murphy* (1940), K brought an action against M, a pools promoter, for £2,497, being the balance of prize money to which K was entitled as winner of the pool. He was unsuccessful, as the action for recovery of a gambling debt could not be entertained in Scotland. In *County Properties & Developments Ltd v Harper* (1989), a croupier made an error by giving an overpayment of gambling chips to a successful customer at a casino. The customer did not count the chips, but continued playing roulette before cashing in the balance. It was held that the encashment of chips was *sponsio ludicra* and the operators of the casino could not recover their loss. In *Ferguson v Littlewoods Football Pools Ltd* (1997), a syndicate of five people completed pools coupons and passed them, with stake money, to a party who failed to pass them to Littlewoods. If the coupons had been received, a dividend of some £2.5 million would have been payable. The syndicate sought payment, but the action was dismissed. They had been staking money on the chance accuracy of football forecasts, which was unenforceable in law. However, in *Robertson v Anderson* (2001), two friends played bingo together. One of them won the national jackpot of £100,000. There was a long standing agreement between the two parties that any winnings would be split both ways. Having established that there was such an agreement, the obvious question was whether it was enforceable. It was held that the agreement was not a gambling debt as it was collateral (connected to, but separate from) the wager itself. It should be added that, in practice, there is considerable statutory control of the gambling industry.

Finally, there is the occasional problem of the so-called "gentleman's agreement" or honourable understanding. In *Ritchie v Cowan & Kinghorn* (1901), R was unable to pay his creditors, C&K, in full but arranged to pay 10s. (50p) in the £1. C&K gave him a receipt on which it stated that they were accepting his payment "in full" but added that it was understood that R would pay the balance "whenever he is able to do so".

It was held that the additional words merely constituted an honourable understanding and were not legally enforceable.

FORMATION OF CONTRACT

A contract is formed (made) when the parties reach agreement on the essential features of the bargain, *i.e.* when they achieve consensus. This does not imply that they must always be in agreement on every minute detail, but it does mean that there has to be agreement on the essentials. The words of Lord President Dunedin in *Muirhead and Turnbull v Dickson* (1905), are often quoted: "commercial contracts cannot be arranged by what people think in their innermost minds. Commercial contracts are arranged according to what people say."

Thus, the law adopts an objective test of whether or not it would appear to the "reasonable man" that agreement has been reached. Basically, contracts are formed by an offer made by one party and an acceptance by the other.

OFFER

To state the obvious, an offer must come before an acceptance. Equally, there can be no acceptance unless there is an offer which is capable of being accepted. The offer may be made verbally, in writing, or by any other suitable means of communication, such as fax, text message or email. Some contracts require to be formed in writing and this is explained in Chapter 2. If the offer is communicated through any of the above means, this is called an *express* offer. The offer may also be inferred from the actings of the parties, *i.e.* the offer is not express, but is by *implication*. If a customer goes into a shop, lifts up an item and hands the money to the sales assistant without saying a word, a valid contract is still formed as both offer and acceptance are implied. Equally, a vending machine (or, rather, the owner of the machine) permanently offers to supply a particular commodity. By placing the appropriate coin in the slot, the consumer implies acceptance. A self-service petrol pump similarly makes an open-ended offer which is accepted by implication when a customer "helps himself".

In *Chapleton v Barry Urban District Council* (1940), C took a deck chair from a stack on the beach which were there on a "help yourself and pay the attendant when he comes round" basis. He was subsequently injured because the chair was defective. It was held that there was a contract between C and the District Council. The pile of deck chairs and the accompanying notice provided an offer by implication. When C helped himself, that was a valid acceptance, also by implication.

Contrast an offer with a willingness to negotiate

A mere proposal to do business is not the same as an offer. Party A might say to party B that he was thinking of selling a particular item of property for £50. If B says "I will take it", is there a contract? The answer would be in the negative and it is important to understand why.

Party A was not making an offer, he was only indicating a willingness to negotiate or extending an "invitation to treat". What B thought was an acceptance was really an offer. Until A accepts the offer, there is no contract. There is one hard and fast rule to which there are no exceptions: *an offer must always come before an acceptance*. To put this another way, no one can accept what is not on offer.

Consider the position of a shopkeeper. When he displays goods in the shop window or on the shelves, what is he doing legally? It is well established in England that shops, in law, do not offer goods for sale; they merely indicate a willingness to negotiate, quite different from the open-ended offer made by a vending machine, referred to above. It is confusing, of course, when shops display signs such as "this week's special offer", when, in fact, they are not offering anything. However, a shop owner does not have to sell any goods against his will and has an absolute right to refuse an offer to buy. In other words, the offer is not made by the seller to sell. The offer is made by the buyer to buy. A shop "is a place for bargaining, not for compulsory sales" (Woolman and Lake, *Contract* (3rd ed., 2001), p.22).

The classic case must be *Pharmaceutical Society of Great Britain v Boots Cash Chemists Southern Ltd* (1952). Legislation required that listed poisons could only be sold under the supervision of a registered pharmacist. Such a poison had been sold in a self-service store. There was no pharmacist near the shelves where the goods were displayed but there was a pharmacist at work beside the cash desk. The question was—when did the actual sale take place? Was it when the customer took the goods off the shelf—or was it when the goods were presented at the cash desk? The court decided that the display of goods on the shelf did not comprise an offer. It was the customer who made the offer by taking the goods to the cash desk. The sales assistant, as agent for the company, accepted the offer and the contract was thus formed, under the supervision of the pharmacist. B was not in breach of the Act. Interestingly, the expressions "cash desk" or "check-out" have tended to be replaced by "point of sale" in recent years. The latter is actually a more accurate legal description. In the subsequent case of *Fisher v Bell* (1961), a shopkeeper displayed a flick knife in his window. Beside the knife was a price ticket bearing the words "ejector knife". It was a statutory offence to sell or offer such a weapon for sale. The shopkeeper's successful defence was that he had not sold nor had he offered to sell the weapon. He had merely indicated a willingness to negotiate, which was not a criminal offence. Subsequent legislation has tended to use expressions such as "unlawful marketing" (*e.g.* Knives Act 1997, s.1(4)) as a catch-all provision.

Other good examples of willingness to negotiate are advertisements or illustrations of goods in catalogues. In 1999, a High Street catalogue chain "offered", in error, on its internet website, television sets at £3.99 instead of £399. People attempted to buy televisions at the low price. The orders were acknowledged by email but "subject to availability". The matter was not tested in court but most legal opinion at the time suggested that there was no contract. The "offer" on the website was merely an invitation to treat. Subsequently, a photographic company mistakenly "offered" a digital camera at a very low price. Customers who applied received an email confirming their orders. The company honoured all such orders placed before the error on the website was corrected. The law on electronic advertisements and offers may not yet be entirely settled.

So, how is it possible to tell whether a particular statement is an offer (in which case it can be accepted) or a mere willingness to negotiate (which cannot be accepted)? In fact, there are no hard and fast rules. It will depend on the facts and circumstances of each individual case. A useful rule of thumb is that if the first party is publicly communicating a statement which is non-discriminatory, that statement is likely to be an offer. Thus the self-service petrol pump offers to supply petrol at the given price to whoever chooses to help himself. A shop keeper, on the other hand, does not, as explained above, have to sell any item of his stock to a customer if he does not wish to.

Quotation of price

If a potential supplier of goods or services indicates the price of his commodity in advance, this will normally be taken to be an estimate or quotation, *i.e.* an indication of willingness to negotiate. In context, however, it could be taken to be a tender or a firm offer. In *Harvey v Facey* (1893), H sent a telegram to F "Will you sell us Bumper Hall Pen?

Telegraph lowest cash price." F telegraphed in reply "Lowest price for Bumper Hall Pen £900." H then telegraphed to F "We agree to buy Bumper Hall Pen for £900 asked by you." H received no reply to his telegram but argued that there was a valid contract. It was held that F's telegram was merely a statement of the lowest price at which he might be prepared to sell. It was not an offer to H nor was it an affirmative reply to the question in H's first telegram. ("Bumper Hall Pen" was the name of a farm in Jamaica. The case came to the Privy Council by way of appeal.)

By contrast, in *Philp & Co. v Knoblauch* (1907), K, a merchant, wrote to P, oil-millers, "I am offering today plate linseed for January/February and have pleasure in quoting you 100 tons at 41/3d usual plate terms. I shall be glad to hear if you are buyers and await your esteemed reply." The following day, P telegraphed "Accept hundred January/February plate 41/3d." The telegram was confirmed by letter. K then attempted to recall his original quotation by sending a telegram to that effect. It was held that K's original letter/quotation was an offer to sell and not merely a statement of the current price. A contract had been formed by P's acceptance telegram even though it did not expressly refer to the condition "usual plate terms" mentioned in the offer. K's subsequent telegram was too late to have any effect.

There are potential problems in this area since the words "offer", "estimate", "quotation" and "tender" are frequently used loosely in colloquial speech. It is a question of interpretation, of the facts and circumstances of each case, as to what the words actually mean in context.

Expression of intention

An announcement by one party that he has something for sale for which offers may be made is normally no more than an indication of willingness to negotiate. In *Paterson v Highland Railway* (1927), the fact that a railway company had announced that reduced rate tickets would be available for a particular period of time did not prevent it from withdrawing the concession before the period expired. In *Mason v Benhar Coal Co.* (1882), the fact that a company had proposed to issue new shares, did not commit it to do so. More recently, in *Dawson International plc v Coats Paton plc* (1993), directors of CP agreed to recommend to company members that an offer from DI to buy their shares should be accepted. The recommendation was duly made but was later withdrawn when a more favourable bid was received from a third party. DI were unsuccessful in their claim for damages for breach of contract since there was no contract. It is not easy to glean precise principles out of the above case law.

If a party invites offers, such as is common in the sale of heritable property, he is not bound to accept any offer, even the highest. When property is advertised at a "fixed price", this is no more than a willingness to negotiate. There is nothing to prevent a prospective buyer from offering a lower or even a higher price. A sale by auction is completed by the fall of the hammer, or equivalent. At this point, the auctioneer, as agent for the seller (exposer), "prefers" (accepts) the highest bid (offer). Until that moment, the bidder may withdraw his offer. In *Fenwick v Macdonald Fraser & Co.* (1904), a case involving the sale of a bull, it was held that the exposer was similarly free to withdraw his goods before the hammer fell. There is English authority in *Barry v Heathcote Ball & Co. (Commercial Auctions) Ltd* (2001) that where there is no reserve price, the highest bid may not be rejected merely because it is not high enough.

Occasionally, the so-called "referential" bid may be encountered in sealed competitive bids, such as an offer to "top" the highest bid by £X or by a given percentage. Bids of this kind were held to be invalid in *Harvela Instruments Ltd v Royal Trust Co. of Canada Ltd* (1986), a House of Lords case, unless the prospective bidders are all given reasonable notice that this method may be employed.

Withdrawal of offer

An offer can be withdrawn, in most cases, at any time before it is accepted. This is an important feature of offers and the period, before acceptance, when the offeror is still free to withdraw is traditionally referred to as *locus poenitentiae* (room for repentance).

If a time limit is placed on the offer and that limit passes without an acceptance, the offer automatically lapses. If an offeror undertakes to keep his offer open for a certain time, this undertaking will be binding upon him. This is because, in Scots law, a promise can be a binding obligation and breach of that promise could give rise to a claim for damages. Promises are further explained in Chapter 2. In *Littlejohn v Hawden* (1882), the solicitor for the seller of an estate indicated by letter that the potential buyer had an option to purchase which would remain open for 10 days. This undertaking was held to be legally binding. If, as in *Effold Properties v Sprot* (1979), the offer simply states that it must be accepted within a certain time, this does not count as an undertaking and the offeror can still withdraw his offer. In formal written offers, it is quite common to find wording such as: "this offer, unless previously withdrawn, remains open for acceptance not later than [...]". Such wording clearly reserves the right to withdraw and puts matters beyond doubt. In *McMillan v Caldwell* (1991), it was held that a formal written offer to buy heritable property can be withdrawn verbally, provided the withdrawal reaches the offeree before he accepts.

How long does an offer last?

When a time limit is stated, the matter is clear. If the offer is not accepted within the time limit, it automatically falls. In many cases there will be no time limit stated. In these circumstances, the offer remains open for a "reasonable" time and what is reasonable depends on facts and circumstances. Clearly there are times when it is only fair to give the second party some days to consider the offer. Equally, there are occasions when it is clear, at least by implication, that an offer must be accepted fairly promptly, *e.g.* if the subject matter is raw materials which have a volatile price movement or where perishable goods are involved.

In the following two cases, the court decided that the original offer had lapsed due to the length of time, *i.e.* it had not been timeously accepted. *Wylie & Lochhead v McElroy & Sons* (1873): an offer to carry out certain iron work on a new building had not been "accepted" until five weeks had passed, during which time there had been a considerable rise in the price of iron. *Glasgow Steam Shipping Co. v Watson* (1873): an offer made on August 5 to supply coal at 7s. (35p) per ton had not been "accepted" until October 13, by which time coal had risen to 9s. (45p) per ton.

In contrast, the court decided in *Murray v Rennie and Angus* (1897), that an offer dated June 10 to carry out certain mason work was still open for acceptance on June 21 and that a valid contract had been formed.

Death, insanity and bankruptcy

Provided the offer has not been accepted, it will automatically lapse on the death, insanity or bankruptcy of the offeror, unless the latter was acting purely as an agent for another party.

ACCEPTANCE

If there is no acceptance of an offer, clearly there can be no contract. It is said that an acceptance must "meet" the offer, *i.e.* there must be consensus. If (and this is quite common) there are new terms or conditions in the so-called acceptance, no contract has yet been formed. What the original offeror has received is confusingly called a "qualified acceptance". It is crucial to note that a qualified acceptance never concludes the process of formation of a contract. This is a rule to which there are no exceptions.

In fact, the so-called qualified acceptance is not an acceptance, as such, but a new offer. This new offer, whether it is called a qualified acceptance or a counter-offer, must in turn be met by an unqualified acceptance before the parties can achieve consensus. Some case law may help to illustrate. *Nelson v The Assets Co. Ltd* (1889): N wrote to A, offering to buy specific parts of a tenement property. A appeared to have accepted the offer "for our interest in the property". On an examination of the title deeds, it was discovered that A did not have a clear title to all of the property in question. N brought an action against A to deliver a valid title. In fact, there was no completed contract of sale as the "acceptance" had been qualified.

Stobo v Morrisons (Gowns) Ltd (1949): an offer was made to purchase a shop and the offer was accepted but "subject to contract". The latter phrase does not have the technical meaning in Scotland that it does in England. In the circumstances of the case, the words "subject to contract" qualified the acceptance and thus there was no concluded contract.

Wolf & Wolf v Forfar Potato Co. Ltd (1984): F offered, by telex, to sell a quantity of potatoes to W, a firm of Amsterdam merchants. The offer was open for acceptance by 5pm on the following day. An "acceptance" was sent by telex from Amsterdam on the following morning, but it contained new conditions. On receipt of the telex, F telephoned W and informed them that the new conditions were unacceptable. W subsequently sent a second telex, still within the time-limit, purporting to accept the terms of the original offer. In fact, no contract existed. The first "acceptance" was a counter-offer, which killed off the original offer. The result was that the original offer was no longer capable of being accepted. The counter-offer or qualified acceptance from W had never been accepted by F. The parties had not achieved consensus.

The acceptance does not require to repeat the offer word for word. It is sufficient that it shows acceptance of the offer as a whole. Like an offer, an acceptance may be either express or implied. In most cases, express acceptance is required in order to achieve consensus but sometimes it may be implied, *e.g.* an order for goods may not require an express acceptance, since acceptance is implied by the very act of supplying the goods. Acceptance can also sometimes be implied from a failure to reject an offer, but this can only arise if there have been similar dealings between the parties in the past. The law, in general, does not take kindly to contracts being imposed on people against their will. The practice whereby certain unscrupulous traders would send unsolicited goods to persons, and demand payment if the goods were not returned within a specified time, was largely curbed by the Unsolicited Goods and Services Act 1971. Persons who receive unsolicited goods can keep these goods if the sender does not take steps to recover them within a certain period.

Method of acceptance
A person making an offer is entitled to state the method by which the acceptance should be communicated, *e.g.* letter, telephone or fax. If the precise method and/or time for acceptance is stated, it must be adhered to. If no special conditions are laid down, acceptance can be given in any competent manner. Usually, it will be given in the same mode as the offer, which is a matter of common sense rather than law.

Offers to the general public
As demonstrated earlier in this chapter, an advertisement is not an offer, merely an indication of a willingness to negotiate. However, there have been rare occasions where the courts have decided that particular advertisements go beyond being mere willingness to negotiate and, in fact, are offers to the general public.

The most celebrated occasion must be *Carlill v Carbolic Smoke Ball Co. Ltd* (1893). CSB, through newspaper advertisements, offered to pay £100 to any member of the public who bought a patent preventative "smoke ball" and, having used it according to instructions, contracted influenza. C bought a smoke ball, used it according to instructions and, not surprisingly, failed to escape influenza. She sought payment of £100 but CSB refused payment, claiming that they had no contract with her. They submitted that the advert was no more than a willingness to negotiate and not an offer and thus could not be accepted. In all the facts and circumstances of the case, the court decided that this particular advertisement was an offer to the general public.

C had accepted the offer when she bought the smoke ball and used it according to the instructions. Accordingly, there was a contract between CSB and C and she was entitled to her payment of £100.

In *Hunter v General Accident, Fire and Life Assurance Corporation* (1909), a coupon policy of insurance in a diary stated that £1,000 would be paid to the representative of any diary owner killed in a railway accident within 12 months of registration with the insurance company. H sent off such a coupon to GA for the purposes of registration. Shortly afterwards, he was killed in a railway accident. GA claimed that the advertisement in the diary had not been an offer, only an indication of willingness to negotiate. H, they claimed, had merely made them an offer, which they had not accepted. There was no argument about the fact that GA had received the coupon from H. The court decided that the publication of the coupon in the diary was an offer and the return of it by H to GA was an acceptance. A valid contract had been formed and H's estate was entitled to the payment of £1,000.

Although the two cases are quite similar, in *Hunter* it was easier to show that a contract had been formed, because GA knew, and admitted they knew, of H's existence. In the case of *Carlill*, CSB had no knowledge of C as an individual. Virtually any book dealing with contract law in the United Kingdom will quote the case of *Carlill*. Nevertheless it is a legal curiosity and somewhat of a maverick case. Today, few commercial organisations would make such undertakings as the ill-fated CSB did in the latter part of Queen Victoria's reign.

Withdrawal of acceptance

The general rule is very simple. Once an acceptance is given, provided it is final and not qualified, it cannot be withdrawn. The parties are now in a mutually binding contract. Under the so-called postal rules (below), there is one interesting and illogical quirk in this rule.

THE POSTAL RULES

Offering and accepting

Where parties are negotiating *entirely* by post, they do not have the advantage of being face to face, or even speaking over the telephone and they have to rely on an agent, *i.e.* the postal service, to convey offers, counter-offers, qualified acceptances and final acceptances. Over the years, certain common law "rules" have grown up but, it is always possible for parties to agree their own provisions or even for certain rules to be inferred.

Starting with the obvious—if an offer is posted, it must actually reach the second party (offeree), otherwise it could not be considered.

The potential problems arise in the case of the acceptance and at what point in time such a posted acceptance actually achieves consensus. It might seem sensible to assume that the contract could not actually be formed until the first party receives the acceptance, but that would not be correct in law. Under the postal rules, consensus is achieved when the second party posts his acceptance. This rule is more logical than it appears. If the offeror makes his offer by post, he is, by implication, appointing the postal service as his agent. When the offeree posts his acceptance he is, in fact, placing it in the hands of the offeror's agent which is as good as placing it in the offeror's own hands. In the absence of any stipulation to the contrary, the offeror is presumed to intend the reply to be made by post. In England, it has been decided that a contract is complete even if the posted acceptance never actually arrives: *Household Fire Insurance Co. v Grant* (1879). It is unlikely that this case would be followed in Scotland.

One of the most unsatisfactory elements of the acceptance rule is that the offeror can actually be in a binding contract, without being aware of it, since the acceptance could have been posted but not yet delivered. It has a further knock-on effect: if an offer is open for acceptance within a specified period, acceptance is effective if it is posted within that time limit. In *Jacobson Sons & Co. v Underwood & Son Ltd* (1894), there was an offer to buy a quantity of straw. The offer stated "for reply by Monday 6th". The acceptance was posted on the 6th but it did not arrive until 7th. The offer had been accepted on time because the reply had been in the hands of the Post Office on the 6th.

It is quite common for parties to contract out of this somewhat tiresome rule and to state in the offer "your reply to be in my hands not later than [...]". This avoids doubt or misunderstanding. Although these rules are called the "postal rules", it is presumed that they would apply to delivery agents, but not to electronic forms of transmission such as fax (see below) or email.

Withdrawal of offer

Human nature being what it is, an offeror might post his offer and then have second thoughts and wish to withdraw it. Following on the principles outlined above, his withdrawal is only effective if it reaches the offeree before the acceptance is placed in the post. *Thomson v James* (1855): J made a written offer to buy an estate from T. Some days later, T posted an acceptance. On the same day on which T posted his acceptance, J posted a letter withdrawing his offer. Both letters were delivered on the following day. In other words, J received an acceptance of the offer which he thought he had withdrawn and T received a withdrawal of the offer which he thought he had accepted. In fact, there was a binding contract since consensus had been achieved when T posted his acceptance. J was too late to withdraw his offer.

Withdrawal of acceptance

From the point of logic, the above rules ought to mean that once an acceptance is posted, it is irrevocable since consensus has been achieved. However, there appears to be a quirk in the law, based on an old case of *Countess of Dunmore v Alexander* (1830). A wrote to D, offering her services as a maid-servant. On November 5, D wrote to A accepting her offer. On the 6th, D changed her mind and wrote to A withdrawing her acceptance. Due perhaps to vagaries of the contemporary postal service,

A received both letters at the same time. For reasons best known to itself, the court decided that D's withdrawal of acceptance was effective; there was no contract. (If the acceptance had reached A before the recall, there would have been a contract.) Over the years, there has been much critical comment about the correctness of this decision and the law report itself is far from clear.

The Scottish Law Commission, Report No.144 (1993), has recommended the abolition of the postal rules and replacement with a rule that once an acceptance has been sent, the offer could not be withdrawn unilaterally. However, an actual contract would only be formed when the acceptance had been communicated to the offeror.

Contracts not covered by the postal rules
In contracts made with overseas parties, if they are made under the Uniform Laws on International Sales Act 1967, the postal rules do not apply. A contract will only be deemed to be completed when an acceptance arrives in the office of the offering party. The postal rules do not apply to communications made by telex which are treated in the same way as oral communications: *Brinkibon Ltd v Stahag Stahl* (1983). Thus an acceptance by telex is effective when it is printed out at the offeror's end. It is assumed that similar rules apply to fax. There are problems, as yet not all resolved, about the so-called "status" of a fax in a contract where offer and acceptance have to be in writing. In these cases, if a faxed acceptance is sent, the original document should, as matter of good practice, be sent on to the offeror without delay. In *McIntosh v Alam* (1998), the sheriff agreed that a faxed copy of a document had no higher status than any other photocopy. Nevertheless, the fact that a particular document had been signed could be communicated by fax, allowing consensus to be achieved, even if the principal copy was not forwarded. Modern technology throws up other problems in the use of email and text messages. An email does not come under the postal rules. Opinion is that an email or text message has to be received, not merely sent. Presumably the recipient would be expected to access the email or text at reasonable intervals. At this point, we are in uncharted waters.

DISTANCE SELLING

Following on the European Community Directive 97/7/EC, the Consumer Protection (Distance Selling) Regulations 2000 (SI 2000/2334) were enacted. They give important protection to buyers of goods or services by means of a "distance contract". A distance contract is one where "consumer" and "supplier" do not have any face-to-face negotiations and would include traditional mail order as well as electronic means such as the telephone, fax, teletext, email and television. The list is not exhaustive. A supplier is someone who acts in a commercial or professional capacity and a consumer is a party who does not act in a business capacity. There are a number of exceptions from regulation including business-to-business transactions and contracts for the sale of land or the provision of financial services.

The broad effect of regulation is that certain basic information about the supplier and the terms of the contract has to be supplied to the consumer. The regulations give the consumer the right, in certain circumstances, to cancel the contract after consensus has been achieved—in effect, a resolutive condition. The consumer can, in any event, withdraw within seven working days and receive a full refund. There are common sense exceptions, such as supply of perishable goods or services which are subject to fluctuation in the financial markets. In cases where the required information has not been given by the supplier, the period is extended to three months. If the supplier does not fulfil the contract within 30 days, the consumer is entitled to a refund unless he elects to accept substitute goods or services.

IMPLIED CONTRACTS

Certain terms or conditions may be implied into a contract by statute. A clear example is a contract for the sale of moveable property which has important statutory terms built in by the Sale of Goods Act 1979. The provisions of the Act are beyond the scope of this book. It would be unusual in the extreme, however, for a court to imply the existence of an entire contract without some overt sign by the parties that they intended to enter into a contractual relationship. However, on occasions, it is both possible and sensible to infer that when two parties took certain actions, it must have been obvious that they intended to form a contract. One (admittedly rare) example is the English case of *Clarke v Dunraven* (1897) in which it was held that competitors in an amateur yacht race had, by entering into the race in terms of the club rules, contracted to pay full compensation to any competitor whose vessel was damaged in the race. Although there was no formal offer and acceptance among each of the members, the court was prepared to imply the existence of contracts.

---

2. PROMISES, WRITING AND PERSONAL BAR

PROMISES

An interesting feature of the Scottish law of obligations is the possibility of having a binding agreement even when nothing is asked in return. It stands to reason that this form of obligation is less common. Most contracts contain an element of reciprocity, *i.e.* both parties are debtor and creditor to one another, so each will give and take something of value. This is usually referred to as "consideration". The tradition, in English law, is that if there is no element of consideration, the contract is not legally enforceable. In *Stilk v Mayrick* (1809), nine seamen had been engaged to sail a ship from London to the Baltic. Two of the crew deserted. The captain promised the remaining seven men that he would pay them extra wages to sail the ship home short-handed but he did not keep his word. The crew were unable to recover the extra money as there was no consideration. They were only doing what they had originally contracted to do, namely to sail the ship.

Scots law follows Roman law in this area. Consideration is not actually a requirement for an undertaking to be legally binding. An obligation to do or give something gratuitously, *i.e.* without asking anything in return, is as enforceable as any mutual contract. In *Morton's Trustees v Aged Christian Friend Society of Scotland* (1899), M wrote to the steering committee for a new charitable society, offering to provide pensions for 50 elderly people. He was to fund this donation by 10 annual capital payments of £100 to the society. His offer was accepted, pensioners were appointed and M duly paid eight of the annual payments but died thereafter, with two payments outstanding. The obligation to meet these two payments was a binding contract and his trustees were liable to make the two outstanding payments.

In law, however, there is a general presumption against donation. In other words, it is presumed that people do not give away anything for nothing. Also, mere verbal promises are not legally enforceable in every case. Under the Requirements of Writing (Scotland) Act 1995, s.1(2)(a)(ii), "writing" is required to constitute a gratuitous unilateral obligation, except where undertaken in the course of a business. Under the pre-1995 law, promises did not require to be in writing to be valid, but could only be proved by what was called the "writ or oath" of the person seeking to deny the existence of the promise. The necessity for proof by writ or oath was abolished retroactively.

A verbal promise can, however, become binding if personal bar operates (see below). It appears that a true gratuitous contract, as distinct from a gratuitous unilateral obligation, does not require to be in writing. What, then, is the difference between the two? In the case of a promise, only one party, the party receiving the promise, has any right to enforce. Furthermore, it seems that a true promise does not require an acceptance to make it enforceable. If it is a gratuitous contract, both parties have rights of enforcement and there will have been an offer and acceptance. This distinction is easier to state than to apply in practice. In *Bathgate v Rosie* (1976), a child accidentally broke a shop window. His mother assured the shop owner that she would pay for the damage, but failed to do so. The sheriff held that she was obliged to pay but, perhaps wisely, did not specify whether, in his opinion, she had made a unilateral promise or entered a gratuitous contract. In *Muirhead v Gribben* (1983), a firm of solicitors assured another firm that the latter's fees would be paid if certain papers were transferred to them. This assurance was held to be contractual. An example of what looked like a promise, but was held to be a contract, can be found in *Petrie v Earl of Airlie* (1834). The Earl had not supported the Reform Act of 1832. Posters appeared accusing him of treasonable conduct. The Earl offered a reward of 100 guineas (£105) for information leading to the detection of the author and printer, the reward to be paid on their conviction. P supplied the required information but the Crown declined to prosecute. The Earl, having himself decided against a private prosecution or civil litigation, was nevertheless obliged to pay the reward to P. A clearer example of a true gratuitous contract can be found in *Wick Harbour Trustees v The Admiralty* (1921): A had undertaken to make certain *ex gratia* payments to W. In his judgment Lord Sands stated that it was a general principle of Scots law that "if a person voluntarily offers to make a payment which he is under no legal obligation to make, and the offer is accepted, that forms a binding contract." Finally, it is worth noting that the use of certain words is not, in itself, conclusive in deciding on the status of any legal undertaking. In *Macfarlane v Johnston* (1864), a company stated by letter "We agree to pay you, during February 1859, £100, during March 1859, £100, during April 1859, £100." In the circumstances, it was held that this was a promise, which did not have to be accepted to be valid. In other words, the legal status of the undertaking was that of a promissory note.

THE REQUIREMENTS OF WRITING

The general rule is that no special formalities are required for parties to enter into a binding contractual obligation. There are, however, exceptions to this general rule and some contracts do require writing for their constitution. Until August 1, 1995, when the Requirements of Writing (Scotland) Act 1995 came into force, there were certain contracts, known as the *obligationes literis*, which required to be expressed in writing as a matter of common law, although the categories were not entirely clear. The law on how documents were validly executed was governed mainly by Acts of the pre-1707 Scots Parliament, as interpreted by the courts over the years, and known by the august collective title of the "Authentication Statutes".

Under the 1995 Act, this entire area of law was modernised. The old common law provisions disappeared, as did the Authentication Statutes. Now, a written document is required, under s.1(2), for: (i) creation, variation or extinction of an interest in land (with the exception of leases of not more than one year's duration); (ii) gratuitous unilateral obligations, unless undertaken in the course of business; and (iii) creation of a trust where a person declares himself to be sole trustee of his own property. There are particular provisions in the Act for the execution of testamentary writings but, as these are not contractual documents, they are not considered further.

Until the 1995 Act came into force, documents which were "holograph" (entirely in the granter's handwriting), or "adopted as holograph", had a privileged status in Scots law. This is no longer the case, nor is there any requirement for documents executed after August 1,

1995 to be holograph or adopted as such. The old rules continue to apply to documents executed prior to the Act coming into force, with one important exception: any rules which stated that certain contracts could only be proved by "writ or oath" disappeared retroactively.

Under the 1995 Act a document is *formally valid if it is subscribed by the granter.* In other words, a simple signature is sufficient formality, on its own, to make the document binding. Thus most contracts only require the signatures of the parties. If a document is to be regarded as self proving (similar to "probative" under the old law) it requires to be attested. This means that it is signed, or the signature is acknowledged, by the granter before one witness aged at least 16 (previously two witnesses were required). When a document is self proving, its subscription is presumed valid without need for further evidence. This does not mean that such a signature is unchallengeable. For example, the signature might be a forgery. It is possible to request the Court of Session to "reduce" a document, which has the legal effect of making it null and void. It is not easy to obtain a decree of reduction on the grounds of faulty or fraudulent execution, since the onus of proof is clearly against the party wishing to reduce. A great advantage of the 1995 Act provisions is that even if the witness's attestation is botched, the document remains formally valid as long as there is a subscription by the granter. The courts also have a statutory power to rectify a defectively expressed document, even if probative or self proving, under the Law Reform (Miscellaneous Provisions) (Scotland) Act 1985. In most cases, only a self proving document can be entered in the public registers. If a document is not self proving, *i.e.* if the signature was not witnessed, an application can be made to the sheriff court to give it self proving status should that be required.

In the case of a basic contract, a signature is required on the last page. Annexations only require to be signed if the contract relates to land. However, an annexation is only incorporated into any contract if it is referred to in the main document and identified on its face as being the annexation referred to. This fairly strict rule applies whether the annexation requires to be signed or not. In practice, it is easy to overlook this requirement.

If a contract is one which requires to be in writing, but is not (or is only partly in writing) and the party "loyal" to the defective contract (*i.e.* who wants it to continue — called the "first party" in the Act) acts, or refrains from acting, with the knowledge and acquiescence of the other party (the "second party"), the latter is said to be *personally barred* from withdrawing from the contract on the grounds of lack of writing. Personal bar will only operate if the position of the first party has been materially affected by his own actings and would be similarly affected if the second party were allowed to withdraw from the contract. This statutory form of personal bar replaced the older common law forms known as *rei interventus* and homologation as a way of "perfecting" a contract which required writing but was lacking in this respect.

There are also statutory instances where certain documents (not all of them contracts) require writing, *e.g.* life assurance, bills of exchange, hire purchase and credit agreements regulated under the Consumer Credit Act 1974.

Parties may, of course, agree between themselves that a contract will be expressed in writing. There are obviously times when such a written agreement is prudent. It could be particularly important to have all the terms and conditions set out clearly in the case of a complex agreement or one which involves substantial obligations. Many people (wrongly, but understandably) perceive a written contract as being more binding than a verbal arrangement and may feel happier to have "something in writing".

In Chapter 1, brief mention was made of electronic means of communicating offers and acceptance in contracts. The Electronic Communications Act 2000 made future provision for electronic communication to be recognised as the equivalent of a written document, including the possibility of electronic signatures.

PERSONAL BAR

Personal bar is a concept which, in some ways, is easier to understand than to explain. At a basic level, the law is concerned with peoples' rights and the necessity to uphold them in a civilised society. However, there could be times where strict enforcement of a right could lead to an injustice. If party A does or says something—and party B acts on that, or if A allows B to do something which A knows he could prevent B from doing—yet does not object, it could be very unjust if A later insists on relying on the true state of affairs. In fact, he would be personally barred from doing so. It is simply a case of the law attempting to be scrupulously fair. Putting it in colloquial terms, A cannot move the goalposts after the game has started.

Personal bar, in addition to the statutory example outlined above, takes a number of different forms, but they all adhere to the same basic idea of fairness.

Holding out

If party A "holds himself out" as being, say, of a certain age and is reasonably believed, he is personally barred from denying that he is of that age in respect of any contract which he enters while giving such an impression. In an old case of *Wilkie v Dunlop* (1834), a minor (as he was then called) booked into an inn. He gave the impression, which was reasonably believed, that he was of full age. He left without paying his bill and was sued by the innkeeper. The young man then indicated that as he was a minor, he could not be sued for the bill (which was legally correct at the time). The court was not impressed with his argument. The minor had held himself out as being of full age and had been reasonably believed. He was personally barred from escaping his liabilities by using the defence of minority. To put it another way, he had given the impression that he was an adult and so, for the purposes of *this* contract, he would be treated as such.

Holding out could also apply in other areas of status, such as partnership or agency. If A says that he is the business partner of B, and B allows A to act as though he is B's partner, B is personally barred from denying that A is his partner if A makes contracts as such. A has held himself out as B's partner, with B's full knowledge. It does not strictly mean that A becomes B's partner, but B has lost the right to deny that A is his partner. Of course, if B did not, and could not reasonably be expected to know of A's actions, B would not be personally barred.

Representation

To paraphrase the words of Lord Birkenhead in *Gatty v MacLaine* (1921), this takes place where party A, either by his words or his actions, justifies B in believing that a certain state of facts exists and B then acts on reliance on these facts to his loss. A is personally barred by representation from stating that the facts were different to those originally stated. Representation is similar to holding out, but relates more to facts than to the status of persons. *London Joint Stock Bank Ltd v MacMillan & Arthur* (1918): a clerk in the employment of M & A approached one of the partners, A, and asked him to sign a cheque for £2 for petty cash. A was in a hurry but, unwisely, signed the cheque. In fact, the cheque was blank apart from the space for figures in which were written "2 0 0"; later, the clerk put a "1" before the "2" and a "0" after it and wrote in the words "one hundred and twenty pounds". The clerk presented the cheque to the bank for payment and absconded with the money. M & A failed in an action against the bank for £118 (the difference between £120 and £2) as it was the firm and not the bank which had acted carelessly and had not taken adequate precautions to prevent forgery. The firm had acted in such a way as to justify the bank in believing that a certain state of affairs existed (that the cheque was for £120) and there was no reason for the bank to be put on its guard. The firm was personally barred by representation from stating later what the true state of affairs was, *i.e.* that the cheque was originally only for £2.

Acquiescence

Acquiescence takes place where a person sees his rights being invaded but takes no action to safeguard them. This lack of action leads other people to believe that he has no objection to the invasion and they make their position accordingly. He is then personally barred by acquiescence from objecting at some later date. An easy example would be failing to object to a nuisance from a neighbour's property. It is of little direct relevance to the everyday law of contract as such, but it can be important in long term continuing obligations affecting heritable property. Property A might be subject to a real burden (explained briefly in Chapter 8), enforceable by the owner of property B, that it can only be used as a private dwelling house. The owner of property A turns the house into a hotel. The owner of property B knows of this invasion of his rights, but takes no action. If he tries, at a later date, to enforce the real burden, he may well be met with a plea that he is personally barred by acquiescence.

Mora and taciturnity

This is closely related to acquiescence and is more relevant to the law of contract. There is no general rule which requires a person to state his objections to another party's actions, or his failure to act, immediately. Nevertheless, he should not delay unduly as he may find himself personally barred. By statute, there are prescriptive periods (see Chapter 10) by which certain rights can be extinguished by a negative prescriptive period of five (in some cases, 20) years if no relevant objection is made. The effect of *mora* and taciturnity is to bar a claim, where a delay in asserting a right may have led the other party to believe that it was not going to be asserted, even when the negative prescriptive period has not run its full length,

In *Pollok v Burns* (1875), P, a habitual drunkard, granted a bill of exchange while quite drunk. He waited six months before challenging the validity of the bill. The challenge failed on the grounds that he had not been so drunk as to be unaware of what he was doing but, in any event, by delaying for six months before making a challenge, he was personally barred on the grounds of *mora* and taciturnity.

Waiver

This is giving up a claim, or an objection, which could otherwise be made. The party who had surrendered the claim or objection would not then be able to found on it.

Notice

Notice is perhaps the simplest form of personal bar. Party A is entitled to assume that what party B tells him is true. However, if A knows perfectly well that what B tells him is untrue, A will not be entitled to act as though he believed it to be true.

Rei interventus, homologation and statutory personal bar

The older textbooks deal with two forms of personal bar known as *rei interventus* and homologation. These were replaced by statutory personal bar, very similar to *rei interventus*, under the Requirements of Writing (Scotland) Act 1995, as explained earlier in this chapter.

3. VALIDITY OF CONTRACTS

When a contract is formed, the parties to it may be completely unaware of any legal requirements. As a result, they may have a contract which is *ex facie* (on the face of it) perfectly valid but which, in some way, is defective. John may be unaware that Trudy is insane. Freda may be unaware that the contract to sell her house to George should be in writing. Depending on the form of the defect, the contract may turn out to be (1) void, (2) voidable or (3) unenforceable. The distinction between these categories is crucial and they will now be separately examined.

Void "contracts"
Basically, a contract is void if, for any reason, the element of consensus is lacking. Strictly speaking, it is illogical to refer to a contract as being void. If a contract is void, there is no contract and there never has been.

Lack of true consent may arise in a number of situations. It might be that one or both of the parties is not recognised in law as having the required capacity (legal capability) to give consent, *e.g.* young children or insane persons. Capacity is dealt with below. Lack of consent could also arise where there is essential error, *e.g.* as to the subject matter of the contract (as in *Raffles v Wickelhaus* (1864) in Chapter 1).

If an apparently valid contract is void, for whatever reason, it has no legal effect and must be treated as though it has never existed. The contract cannot (obviously) be enforced by the courts.

Third parties may also be affected if a contract is void. Even though third parties act in good faith and without knowledge of its nullity, they cannot acquire any rights through it. Thus, if Smith sells goods to Jones and the contract of sale is void, to whom do the goods belong? The answer is easy. They still belong to Smith, because there is no contract.

What if Jones meantime had sold goods to Brown (the third party), who paid for them and acted in good faith. To whom do they then belong? The answer is the same. They still belong to Smith, thus Brown must return them to Smith. Brown, of course, can sue Jones for damages, but the fact remains that the ownership of the goods cannot pass to the third party. A very simple example of a void contract is where the subject matter is stolen goods, in which case the stolen goods will always belong to their original owner no matter how much time has elapsed nor on how many occasions they have changed hands, even if in good faith.

In *O'Neil v Chief Constable of Strathclyde* (1994), one car was exchanged (bartered) for another car which turned out to have been stolen. The car which had *not* been stolen was sold to a third party who took in good faith and for value. Because one stolen car had been involved, the original contract of barter was void. The third party could not acquire rights to the non-stolen car.

Voidable contracts

If a defect in a contract does not strike at the root of the agreement and does not, therefore, remove the basic consensus, the contract is not void, merely voidable. A contract could also be voidable because of some defect in its formation, *e.g.* if a contract for the sale of a house is not in writing, as explained in Chapter 2. The contract, as it stands, is not invalid and it could still be honoured by the parties to it, or personal bar might operate.

In other words, if a contract is voidable, it is valid until steps are taken to have it set aside or "avoided", which basically means cancelled. The parties have two options: either they can ignore the defect and treat the contract as fully binding or one of them can use the defect as a means of setting the contract aside.

A particularly important point to notice is the different position of third parties when compared with void contracts. If goods, property or rights which have changed hands under a voidable contract are subsequently transferred to a third party, that party does acquire ownership of them, so long as he has acted in good faith and for value and, at the time of transfer, the original contract has not been avoided. Taking the example above and substituting voidable for void, Brown, the third party acting in good faith and for value, would be able to obtain ownership of the goods.

The right to cancel (avoid, reduce, set aside) a voidable contract may be lost in certain cases, such as where the parties cannot restore each other to their former positions, known as *restitutio in integrum* (entire restoration). As indicated above, a third party cannot be required to give up goods acquired in good faith and for value. This has a further important knock-on effect. If the third party has acquired goods in such a manner, the original voidable contract can no longer be set aside. Personal bar may also operate to prevent the contract being avoided.

Unenforceable contracts

These are contracts which are not necessarily void nor voidable but, because of their nature, cannot be enforced in the courts. The most obvious examples are social agreements and *sponsiones ludicrae*, mentioned in Chapter 1. These contracts may be perfectly valid, but the courts will not enforce them. In the case of *Robertson v Balfour* (1938), R placed two bets with B, a bookmaker, on two horses. Both horses won. R received £10 to account of total winnings of £43 10s and agreed not to insist on the balance for a fortnight. The balance was not paid. B agreed that the debt was due but, as a gambling debt, it was unenforceable at law, but not invalid nor illegal.

FACTORS AFFECTING VALIDITY

The main reasons for a contract being either void or voidable (apart from the requirements of writing considered in Chapter 2) are: lack of contractual capacity, error, misrepresentation and illegality. These factors will be considered in turn in the remainder of this chapter and in Chapters 4, 5 and 6.

CONTRACTUAL CAPACITY

The capacity, *i.e.* the legal capability, of certain persons to make a contract may be limited either at common law or by statute, because it is considered, for one reason or another, that they cannot, or should not be able to, give valid consent.

Children and young people
The Age of Legal Capacity (Scotland) Act 1991, came into force on September 25, 1991. The Act was not retrospective and the basic civil and personal rights of children were not affected. The basics of the law before and after the coming into force of the Act will now been considered.

The old law
Scotland followed Roman law and divided young people into two groups: pupils (girls under 12, boys under 14) and minors (girls 12 to 18, boys 14 to 18). Pupils had no contractual capacity, apart from an obligation to pay a fair price for "necessaries". Contracts were made for them by their tutors, usually father or mother. Minors had limited capacity in that they could make contracts with the consent of their curators, usually father or mother. There were exceptions, *e.g.* if necessaries were supplied, the young person had to pay a fair price. If a minor had no parents and no curator, he enjoyed full contractual capacity. A minor in business on his own had full capacity as had a minor who was "forisfamiliated" (emancipated from his family), *e.g.* married and/or living away from home or serving in the armed forces. In *McFeetridge v Stewarts & Lloyds* (1913), M, a 16-year-old Irish labourer, was injured at work and accepted a compensation payment which was not over-generous. He later tried to overturn his own acceptance on the grounds of age, but was unable to do so as he was forisfamiliated. Pupils and minors could challenge contracts made on their behalf during pupillarity or minority if it could be shown that such contracts had caused them "enorm lesion" (substantial harm). The challenge had to take place not later than four years after attaining majority. This period was known as the *quadriennium utile* (useful four years). Contracts made by a minor himself in the course of trade or business could not be challenged in this way. Rights which vested prior to 1991 are not affected but, with the progress of time, are of declining relevance.

The new law
The old division of young people under the age of majority into two separate categories disappeared and a new single tier system took its place. Young people under the age of 16 ("children") have no contractual capacity subject to certain exceptions. So, "reasonable transactions"

commonly entered into by persons of their age and circumstances are valid (s.2(1)). These reasonable transactions would include children buying items such as sweets or travelling on a bus. Under the old law, these transaction were all, in theory, void unless it could be shown that they were necessary. A positive aspect of the 1991 Act is that it builds in an element of flexibility through age and circumstances, recognising that growing up is a gradual process. A nine-year-old is unlikely to be spending large sums of money, whereas a 15-year-old could have substantial spending power.

Young people aged 16 and 17 have full contractual capacity, although transactions which cause them "substantial prejudice" may be set aside on application to the court. The young person has until age 21 in which to apply, so the period within which the challenge may be made ranges from three to five years, depending on circumstances. The court would only set aside a transaction if (s.3(2)) an adult exercising reasonable prudence would not have entered into it and it has caused, or is likely to cause, substantial prejudice to the applicant. This does not imply that any contract which does not work out as well as expected can be easily set aside. Similarly, if a young person aged 16 or 17 engaged in business or trade makes a contract in that connection, it is unlikely that he will easily be able to plead substantial prejudice. Also, if a young person held himself out as being of full age and was reasonably believed, he could be personally barred. Challenges available at common law, *e.g.* error, fraud, facility and circumvention or undue influence are not affected.

Parties might well be ultra-cautious about entering into a transaction with any young person aged between 16 and 17, particularly if buying heritable property. Section 4 introduces a procedure for making a proposed transaction unchallengeable by judicial ratification. This is achieved by joint action under summary cause and the sheriff's decision is final. There is an element of doubt as to exactly what is meant by "proposed". It seems that judicial ratification cannot be sought retrospectively. There is no provision under the new law for any challenge to a bad bargain made on behalf of a child by a parent or guardian. A child may sue the parent or guardian for damages but could not set the bad bargain aside.

Under an amendment to the 1991 Act, introduced by the Children (Scotland) Act 1995, a person under the age of 16 has the legal capacity to instruct a solicitor in connection with any civil matters where that young person has a general understanding of what it means to do so. A person aged 12 years or more is presumed to have such an understanding.

Insane persons
An insane person (and insanity is not always a very precise concept at common law) has no capacity to contract although he must pay a reasonable price for "necessaries". The contract will be void, even if one party is unaware that the other is insane, as was the case in *Loudon v Elder's Curator* (1923). Traditionally, someone certified insane might

have had a *curator bonis* (one who has a care of goods) appointed by the court and all contracts would made through him. Most of the provisions of the Adults with Incapacity (Scotland) Act 2000, are now in force. Incapacity is defined as an inability through mental disorder or physical disability to act, make, communicate, understand or retain the memory of decisions. Depending on circumstances a guardian, intromitter or intervener can be appointed and applications for appointment of a *curator bonis* are now incompetent. A fundamental principle of the Act is that there must be no intervention unless it is for the benefit of the adult and the outcome cannot be achieved in any other way. So far as is reasonably possible, the views of the adult must be taken into account. Furthermore any intervention must take the least restrictive option. Thus the Act provides for the sheriff to grant an intervention order which will permit the sale or disposal of property, including a house, without the need to go for a full guardianship order.

At common law, when a person suffers from mental illness with some lucid moments, he will be bound by contracts made during these intervals. Given the new statutory definition of incapacity, it seems less likely that a claim that a decision was made during a lucid interval will succeed.

When a person who is involved in a continuing contract (*e.g.* a partner in a firm) subsequently becomes insane, the contract is not automatically invalidated. Thus a partnership is not dissolved merely by the insanity of a partner, although his insanity would be a ground for the court to dissolve the firm (Partnership Act 1890, s.35).

Under the Law Reform (Miscellaneous Provisions)(Scotland) Act 1990, s.71, a power of attorney signed after January 1, 1991 will continue in force, even if the granter subsequently becomes mentally incapable. The provision is not retroactive.

In law, there is a presumption of sanity. The contrary must be proved or admitted.

Intoxicated persons
Intoxication, like insanity, is a question of fact and degree. As a general rule, drunkenness is not a ground on which a contract is either void or voidable unless the drunkenness has reached the stage where the person has lost his reason and could give no true consent.

A contract made when a person is in such a state is theoretically voidable, but only if he takes steps to do so as soon as he recovers his senses and realises what he has done (see *Pollok v Burns* (1875) in Chapter 2). Delay in attempting to avoid the contract will likely result in his being personally barred from doing so, on the grounds of *mora* and taciturnity. *Taylor v Provan* (1864): in the course of a day, P visited T's farm and offered to buy 31 cattle, first at £13 10s. (£13.50), then £13 15s.(£13.75) and finally at £14 each. T refused to sell for less than £15. P then tried, without success, to buy cattle elsewhere. That same evening, somewhat worse for drink, P returned to T and offered him £15 per head, which was accepted. Subsequently, P claimed that he had been incapable, by virtue of

intoxication, of entering the contract. As there was no evidence to show that
P had been totally incapacitated by intoxication, the contract was held to be
valid. Provan "was in such a condition from drink that he had not all his wits
about him[....]and if that were sufficient ground for annulling a bargain, I
fear we would have plenty of reductions" (Lord Justice-Clerk Inglis). In fact,
there is no modern Scottish case in which a contract has been set aside on the
grounds of intoxication.

Enemy aliens

An alien (*i.e.* a person who is not a United Kingdom or Commonwealth
citizen) normally has full contractual capacity in the United Kingdom
during peacetime. This is irrespective of the position in his own home
country, unless the U.K. party was aware of a lack of capacity (Contracts
(Applicable Law) Act 1990, s.2). The position is quite different in the
case of an enemy alien. Such a person only emerges in times of actual
war. If there is a state of war between the United Kingdom and another
country, anyone who voluntarily resides or carries on business in that
country, or in territory occupied by it, is counted as an enemy alien. It
does not matter what his original nationality is; he could even be British.
It is illegal to make contracts with him and any existing contracts are
considered void, at least during the period of hostilities. At the end of the
war, the rights of the parties revive, although the original contract
probably will not be performed. *Cantiere San Rocco v Clyde Shipbuilding
and Engineering Co. Ltd* (1923): an Austrian company had, in May 1914,
entered into a contract with a Scottish company for the supply of marine
engines for £11,550, to be paid by instalments. The Austrians paid the
first instalment of £2,310 in May 1914. Some work was done but the
contract could not be taken further due to the outbreak of war. After the
war, the Austrians brought an action for repayment of the instalment they
had paid. They could not, strictly speaking, recover this money under the
law of contract, as the original contract no longer existed. They were,
however, entitled to recover the instalment by "restitution" on the
principle of *causa data causa non secuta* (consideration given, but
consideration not followed).

Corporate bodies

Corporate bodies are sometimes referred to as artificial or juristic or non-
natural persons, *i.e.* they are recognised in law as persons who have
capacity to contract, but they are obviously not "people", in the normal
sense of that word. The capacity of the body will vary according to its
constitution.

If it was constituted by Royal Charter, the Charter itself may provide
which types contract may be formed. In practice, such a body would be able
to enter into any contract not expressly forbidden. In the case of a body set
up by statute, provision will be found in the relevant statute and, possibly, in
delegated legislation. In the previous two examples, if such a body purports

to do something not permitted under its constitution, it is said to be acting *ultra vires* (beyond the powers). Contracts which are *ultra vires* are void and cannot be made valid even with the consent of all members of the body. The most common form of corporate body is the limited company. Historically, a company was bound by the "objects" of the company (the reason for the formation of the company and what its ongoing purposes and powers were) as set out in its memorandum of association. So far as third parties are concerned, the doctrine of *ultra vires* is now only of historical interest in the case of registered companies. As a result of the Companies Act 1989, ss.108-110, any outside party contracting with a company need not be concerned about its capacity to contract.

Because corporate bodies are non-natural persons, contracts have to be made on their behalf by agents such as directors, office bearers or managers.

Unincorporated bodies
Unincorporated bodies, such as many clubs, associations and churches, do not have a separate personality in law from those who make them up. There is an important exception to this rule in the case of Scottish business partnerships, for which see below. An unincorporated body cannot make contracts or be sued in its own name, only in the name of its trustees or office bearers. Thus, the capacity of an unincorporated body is nil, although from a practical point of view, the capacity of its office bearers is what matters. When three office bearers signed a promissory note "on behalf of the Reformed Presbyterian Church, Stranraer", they were personally liable, since the Church was an unincorporated body and totally lacked contractual capacity (*McMeekin v Easton* (1889)).

Partnerships
In Scotland, a partnership ("firm") has a distinct legal personality of its own, even although it is not incorporated (Partnership Act 1890, s.4(2)). A partner in a firm is the agent both for the firm and for his fellow partners. Every partner is liable jointly and severally for all the debts of the firm. Thus an unpaid creditor, after he has first sued the firm and not received full satisfaction, can sue any one of the partners for the full outstanding debt. This partner is then entitled to claim *pro rata* (proportionate) relief from the other partners.

The acts of the partners, in carrying on the usual business of the firm are binding on that firm, provided they are within its normal scope and objects—and also provided there is nothing to put a third party on his guard. A partner in a business firm has implied authority to borrow money in the firm name, again provided there is nothing to put a prospective lender on his guard. In *Paterson Bros v Gladstone* (1891), the firm of P, builders and joiners, had three partners, R, W and J. W took full charge of finance. R took out a loan and granted security in the firm name through G, a moneylender, at 40% interest. R then misappropriated the loan. The firm was not liable to repay G, since the loan had been granted in suspicious circumstances. A

business firm could easily have obtained a regular loan at a much lower rate
of interest. G (the third party) was a moneylender, well experienced in
financial matters. He ought to have been put on his guard.

Limited liability partnerships

The Limited Liability Partnership Act 2000 created a new legal body, the
limited liability partnership ("LLP"). An LLP is a legal person, separate
from its members combining the organisational flexibility of a traditional
partnership but allowing limited liability for its members. Contractually,
an LLP has the capacity to contract as if it were a natural person. It would
do so through its members, as agents for the LLP.

Agents

An agent is a person who has been authorised by another (the "principal")
to act on his behalf in forming contracts with third parties. The agent will
not wish to be a party to the contract but will bring the principal and the
third party into a contractual relationship. The capacity of an agent cannot
exceed that of his principal.

An agent may be said to have *actual* authority, and this actual authority
may be either express or implied. A third party is entitled to presume that an
agent has the normal powers that an agent in his position would usually
have, unless there is something to put him on his guard. In the latter case, the
third party cannot be said to be acting in good faith until he satisfies himself
on this matter. So, provided an agent is acting within the normal area of
authority of a person in his position, he can bind his principal contractually,
even although the principal may not have authorised what he has done. This
is always subject to the third party having acted in good faith.

There can even be times when an agent has been expressly forbidden
from forming certain contracts or has had some unusual restriction placed on
his authority—and yet, he can still contractually bind his principal. Provided
the agent acts within the normal scope of an agent of his type and the third
party has no knowledge of the restriction, or is not put on his guard, the
agent can bind his principal. This is called *apparent* or *ostensible* authority.
The agent has no authority at all; he only appears to have it. Although the
contract between the agent and the third party is valid, the agent may still be
liable in damages to his principal for disobeying his clear instructions. In
Watteau v Fenwick (1893), the manager of a public bar was instructed not to
buy supplies for use in the bar. This was an unusual restriction. A cigar
salesman, who knew nothing of this arrangement, came into the bar and, in
good faith, sold the manager a quantity of cigars for resale. The bar owner
refused to pay for them, claiming that the manager had no authority to buy
such supplies. Since the third party (the cigar salesman) had no notice of the
restriction and there was nothing to put him on his guard, the contract was
valid. The bar manager had acted within his ostensible authority. His
principal, the bar owner, was contractually bound.

4. THE EFFECT OF ERROR ON CONTRACTS

Either, or both, parties to a contract may have entered into it under some form of error and this may well affect the validity of the contract. In the first instance, errors can be divided into two distinct categories:

Errors as to law

These could arise where one or other of the parties was in error in relation to his rights or to the legal effect of the contract. The general rule is that an error as to law does not affect the validity of a contract. There is a well known legal maxim *ignorantia juris neminem excusat* (ignorance of the law is no excuse). However, it is worth noting that, as a result of the case of *Morgan Guaranty Trust of New York v Lothian Regional Council* (1995), it seems to be established that where a *payment* is made under error of law it can be recovered. However, such a claim for "repetition" (repayment) is not strictly part of the law of contract, rather it is available as an equitable remedy known as the *condictio indebiti* (a claim for repayment of money paid in the mistaken belief that it was due).

Errors as to fact

One or both of the parties may be mistaken as to some fact connected with the contract, *e.g.* the price of the goods. Errors as to fact can affect the validity of a contract in different ways. What follows hereafter is an examination of the legal effect of errors of fact, in different situations.

ERROR OF EXPRESSION

Errors of expression can arise where there is no doubt what both parties meant but, owing to a clerical error of a third party, the written contract is not expressed in the terms originally agreed by the parties. In *Anderson v Lambie* (1954), the owner of an estate, of which a farm formed part, agreed to sell only the farm. Due to a mistake by his solicitor, the entire estate was conveyed to the buyer. As the disposition (the deed which conveys heritable property) did not give effect to the original agreement, the court reduced the disposition so that a new one, which would only include the farm, could be recorded in its place. *Krupp v John Menzies Ltd* (1907) S.C. 903, is a case which perpetuates an unfortunate clerk's arithmetical error. K was the manager of a hotel, owned by J. At the time of her appointment there was verbal agreement that, in addition to a basic salary, she would be paid 1/20th of the net annual profit of the hotel. A clerk was instructed to draw up a written agreement and he was given an old contract, referring to another hotel, to use as a style. In this old contract, the manager's share was shown as 1/10th of the net annual profits, but the clerk was told to *halve* this amount in the case of K's contract. The clerk was unable to calculate 1/2 of 1/10th and, by mistake, he inserted the figure of 1/5th in K's contract. After working for J for some years, K sued for payment of her share of the profits, claiming

1/5th, as expressed in the written contract, rather than the 1/20th which had originally been agreed verbally. J was allowed to bring evidence to show what the original agreement between the parties had actually been. In the more recent case of *Aberdeen Rubber Ltd v Knowles & Sons (Fruiterers) Ltd* (1995), a disposition conveyed an area of ground not included in the original missives (contract of sale of heritable property). There were informal communications between the parties (*i.e.* apart from the missives) which might have been taken to include the additional area. The missives themselves were clear. It was held that the disposition proceeded, mistakenly, on the informal communications, which themselves contained a mistake. The disposition was reduced in respect of the affected area.

In some ways, this type of error is not so much an error of fact as a defect in the way in which the contract is expressed. At common law, there is equitable power to deal with such situations by reducing the written document entirely, as demonstrated in the three cases above. This can only take place after an action of reduction in the Court of Session. There is a simpler statutory procedure under the Law Reform (Miscellaneous Provisions)(Scotland) Act 1985, ss.8 and 9 to rectify documents which fail to express what the parties intended. In practice, the statutory procedure is more usual than the common law action of reduction and tends to be less expensive. Another advantage of the statutory procedure is the power given to the court to change the wording of a document. At common law, the court can basically uphold or reduce a document (or parts of it) but cannot change it. A statutorily rectified document is, to all intents and purposes, counted as though it had always been in its rectified state. There is protection of third parties who have acted in good faith in reliance on the document in its original state.

Error of expression can also occur when a person expresses an offer in terms which he did not intend and the incorrect offer is accepted; an example would be quoting a lower price than intended. If the person accepting the offer knows that there is a mistake, the contract is probably void. If he does not know of the mistake, the position is less clear and all one can say is that the contract could be voidable in some circumstances. In *Seaton Brick and Tile Co. Ltd v Mitchell* (1900), a contractor was held to be bound by a tender which had been based on his own miscalculations. However, in *Wilkie v Hamilton Lodging-House Co. Ltd* (1902), a joiner offered to do certain work at "schedule rates" but undercharged his total bill through a miscalculation which was obvious on the face of the document; he was entitled to charge the full amount. This matter is also considered under "unilateral error" below.

If there is a faulty transmission of an offer, there will be no contract if the message delivered is substantially different from the original. In these days of fax and email, such problems are less common than they were when telegrams were sent down land-lines in Morse code. In *Verdin Bros v Robertson* (1871), R sent a telegram from Peterhead to V in Liverpool: "Send on immediately fifteen/twenty tons salt invoice in my name". When the telegram was delivered in Liverpool, it read "Send on rail immediately fifteen/twenty tons salt Morice in morning name". V sent on salt and invoices to "Morice, Peterhead". V subsequently brought an unsuccessful action for the price against R. Due to the faulty transmission of the offer by telegram there was no consensus and thus no contract.

ERROR OF INTENTION

For there to be an error of intention, one or both of the parties must be mistaken as to the nature or subject matter of the contract which they are entering. This area can be divided into three aspects: (1) unilateral error, (2) common error and (3) mutual error (incidental and essential).

UNILATERAL ERROR

The general rule is that if the error is of one party only, this does not affect the validity of the contract. So, if a person with full contractual capacity freely and willingly pays more for something than it is worth or sells something for less than its true value, the contract cannot be set aside on these grounds alone provided the party was not induced to enter the contract by fraud or misrepresentation. In *Stewart v Kennedy* (1890), S agreed to sell heritable property to K, but because the property was subject to an entail, its sale had to be "subject to the ratification of the court". S thought this phrase meant that the court would decide if the price was fair and reasonable, which was not so. This error on S's part would only be a ground for reducing the contract if it could be shown that the error was induced. In *Spook Erection (Northern) Ltd v Kaye* (1990), a business mistakenly believed that a property it was selling was subject to a 990 year lease, whereas it was only for 90 years. As there was no misrepresentation, the contract was valid. The above rule that unilateral uninduced error does not invalidate a contract finds one exception in the case of gratuitous contracts.

However, this area of law is not without some element of controversy. Unilateral error could be relevant where the other party *knew* that a mistake had been made but was prepared to take unfair advantage. In some ways, this could be considered as an error of expression (dealt with above) except that, in traditional terms, error of expression occurs where a mistake is made in a written document, but the parties were originally in agreement. In *Steuart's Trustees v Hart* (1875), a seller of land believed that it was burdened with an annual feu-duty of £9.75, whereas the true amount was 15p, making the capital value of the land considerably greater. The buyer knew the correct amount of feu-duty; he also knew of the seller's mistake. The court reduced the contract of sale on the grounds of essential error (explained further below). This case was cited with approval in *Angus v Bryden* (1992), where the seller of certain fishing rights on the River Ayr intended to convey only the river fishings and not the sea fishings—which he also owned. However, the actual decision in favour of the seller hinged on a different point of law. It is a somewhat different matter if one side makes a mistake, but the other party genuinely does not know of it. In *Steel's Trustee v Bradley Homes* (1972), one party agreed in writing to receive an interest payment on money, but unknown to the other party, had intended to request payment from two years earlier than the agreement provided. The contract stood.

BILATERAL ERROR AND ERROR OF INTENTION

Both common error and mutual error, which are dealt with below, are sometimes said to be forms of bilateral error. The latter is a somewhat misleading term as it could be taken to imply that both parties must be in error, which, as will become obvious, is not always the case. If parties are genuinely at cross purposes, they need not both be in error. Where both parties are in error, or have so confused the situation that they cannot have achieved consensus, these situations are more accurately classified as errors of intention.

COMMON ERROR

Common or shared error can arise when both parties have made the *same* mistake about a matter of fact. To put it another way, they both share the same mistaken belief. If the error is material and goes to the root of the contract, that contract will be void. A statutory example is where there is a contract of sale of specific goods, *e.g.* a particular painting, which, unknown to the seller, have perished at the time the contract is made. In such circumstances, the contract is void (Sale of Goods Act 1979, s.6).

However, where the common error was really just a matter of opinion, as distinct from an error of fact, the contract will be valid. In *Dawson v Muir* (1851), M sold certain vats to D for £2. Both parties were of the opinion that they were only of scrap value. Subsequently, it was found that they contained white lead, valued at £300. M wished the contract to be set aside but, as there was no error of fact, the contract stood. Similarly, the contract stood in *Leaf v International Galleries* (1950), when both buyer and seller mistakenly, but genuinely, believed that a particular painting was a genuine work of John Constable.

MUTUAL ERROR

This refers to a situation where, for reasons good or bad, the parties have misunderstood one another. Each party thinks consensus has been achieved, but each has a different perception of what has been agreed. In such a situation, the courts will have to look at the terms of any written contract or the prior negotiations.

If the misunderstanding does not go to the heart or root of the contract, *i.e.* is "incidental", the contract will stand unless the error was induced by misrepresentation, in which case, the contract may be voidable. If, however, the error goes to the root of the contract *i.e.* is "essential" (of the essence), the contract is void.

Incidental error

Confusingly, this can also be referred to as *error concomitans* (collateral error). As indicated above, this form of error refers only to matters which do not go to the root of the contract or are only incidental. Such incidental errors do not prevent basic consensus and therefore the contract will stand, unless the error was induced by misrepresentation, in which case the contract may be voidable. In *Cloup v Alexander* (1831), the manager of a company of French comedians hired an Edinburgh theatre "for their performances". The comedians subsequently discovered that it was illegal for them to present their performances in that particular theatre. They were still obliged to pay the rent. The error in this case was a secondary or collateral issue, namely what kind of act could be put on in the theatre. The essential part of the contract was the hire of the building, which had been done without any reference to the kind of act which was to be performed. Furthermore, there had been no misrepresentation on the part of the owners of the theatre.

Essential error

Also known as error *in substantialibus* (in the substantials) this is error that is material and goes to the root of the contract. As the error is of the essence of the contract, there is no consensus—which makes the contract void, not merely voidable. Error is said to be essential "whenever it is shown that but for it one of the parties would have declined to contract"— Lord Watson in *Menzies v Menzies* (1893). Traditionally, essential error occurs in five possible situations, although these should not be regarded as final or watertight.

Subject matter

This arises when the parties believe they are in agreement as to which item or service forms the subject matter whereas, in fact, they have different things in mind. One of the classic cases is *Raffles v Wichelhaus* (1864), which was considered in Chapter 1. In *Scriven v Hindley* (1913), a bidder at an auction sale put up a bid for a barrel which he thought contained hemp. In fact, it contained considerably cheaper tow. The bidder was not bound by the contract.

Price

The fact that a price has not been fixed does not make a contract void as a matter of course. If it has not been fixed (or some clear reference system put in place to ascertain the price), this usually means that the parties are still at the pre-contract stage of negotiation. However, it is possible for both parties to think that a price has been fixed whereas, in fact, they have different prices in mind. In such circumstances, the contract will be void. This is all very well on paper, but there may be practical problems, the most obvious being that the goods may have been consumed or be in such a condition that it is impracticable to return them to their original owner. If the goods cannot be returned, the courts have power both at common law and by statute (Sale of Goods Act 1979, s.8) to fix a reasonable price. In *Stuart & Co. v Kennedy* (1885), an order was placed for a quantity of coping stone, the price being agreed at so much per foot. When the buyer received his bill, he had been charged £77 more than he had expected. It transpired that one of the parties had calculated the price by reference to lineal feet, while the other had calculated it by reference to square feet. As there was no consensus, the contract was void. It was not practicable to dig up and return the coping stone and so the original buyer had to pay the market price for it. In *Wilson v Marquis of Breadalbane* (1859), there was a genuine misunderstanding about the price of cattle being sold by W to M. W thought that the agreed price was £15 per head, whereas M thought they had agreed £13. The contract was void but M elected to keep the cattle. The court required him to pay the current market price which, unfortunately for him, was fixed at £15 per head.

Identity

In many cases, it matters little with whom a party actually contracts. However, there are times when identity can be of the essence of a contract. There are certainly cases where *delectus personae* (choice of person) applies. Common sense indicates that if A wants his portrait painted by X, he need not accept a portrait painted by Y. But, in the case of less personal contracts, what would be the effect of B thinking that he is contracting with C but, in fact, is contracting with D? Is there a contract at all? The contract will be void if, but only if, personal identity is of the essence of that particular contract.

In *Morrisson v Robertson* (1908), a confidence trickster named Telford ("T") introduced himself to M, a cattle dealer, fraudulently claiming to be the son of Wilson of Bonnyrigg, a dairy farmer of good credit, who was known to M. T, alias Wilson, also claimed that he had been given authority by his father to buy two cows from M on "the usual credit terms". M was totally deceived and gave the cows to T without hesitation, on the basis of Wilson of Bonnyrigg's good standing. T had no intention of paying for the cows. He sold them on to a third party, R, who bought in good faith, without knowing that they had been improperly obtained. When M realised that he had been tricked, he made enquiries and found that the cows were in R's possession. T had disappeared by this time and there was no immediate prospect of raising an action against him. M sued R for the return of the cows. The original contract between M and T was void because of the error in M's mind as to the true identity of T. The latter had never owned the cows and so he could not pass ownership to R, the third party, even though R had acted in good faith. The cows still legally belonged to M, who was entitled to recover them. R was entitled to sue T for return of his money.

This case should be contrasted with *MacLeod v Kerr* (1965). K advertised his car for sale. A con-man named Galloway, who told K his name was Craig, responded to the advertisement and agreed to buy the car. He wrote out a cheque for the required amount and signed it "L Craig". K gave G the registration document and G drove the car away. When K presented the cheque it was dishonoured by the bank, as it was from a stolen chequebook and the signature was a forgery. The police were informed. A few days later, Galloway, now giving his name as Kerr, sold the car to Gibson, a garage proprietor, who bought in good faith. Galloway was subsequently arrested and convicted of certain criminal charges. The question now to be resolved was the ownership of the car. MacLeod, the procurator fiscal, raised an action of multiplepoinding to allow the civil courts to decide on the matter. K argued that there had been essential error of identity, which made the original contract void. If he had succeeded in such a submission, the car would still have belonged to him. However, the court held that the car belonged to Gibson, the third party. The original contract between K and Galloway had not been void, merely voidable. When the contract was formed, there was no error in K's mind as to the identity of the person with whom he was contracting: it was the man in front of him, whether he called himself Galloway or Craig. This was not a case of essential error as to the identity of the party, so *Morrisson v Robertson* was not applied. Even although the original contract had been voidable through induced incidental error, it could no longer be set aside, because the third party (Gibson) had acquired rights.

It is probably fair comment to suggest that the courts today are more likely to follow *MacLeod v Kerr* than *Morrisson v Robertson*. Where parties negotiate face to face—and even where the con-man claims to be a named or well known individual—the courts tend to the view that the identity of the confidence trickster is not of the essence of the contract.

In two English cases involving identity, contracts were held to be voidable. In *Phillips v Brooks* (1919), a trickster visiting a jeweller's shop claimed to be Sir George Bullough. The shop owner checked a directory and found that there was such a person at the address given and allowed the trickster to take away a ring on credit. In *Lewis v Averay* (1971) a con-man obtained credit by claiming to be the actor Richard Greene (best remembered for his role as "Robin Hood") and by producing a Pinewood Studios card.

Quantity, quality or extent

Some authorities take the view that this is really just another example of error as to the subject matter (above) rather than a distinct category of its own. It would not be relevant, of course, where people make the same mistake, as that would be common error as in *Leaf v International Galleries* (1950) above. In *Patterson v Landsberg & Son* (1905), P, herself a dealer, bought from a London dealer certain items of jewellery, which appeared to be antique. In fact they were reproductions. The contract was void. There had been a crucial misunderstanding as to the quality of the goods.

Nature of the contract

It seems that this kind of error can only arise in the case of a written contract. It could arise when a party signs a document which he did not intend, or in a way in which he did not intend, such as signing as a witness, only to find that he was a party to the deed. In *McLaurin v Stafford* (1875), a party thought he was signing a will. In fact, he was signing a document giving away his property there and then.

However, the law is not generally sympathetic to individuals who, without being induced by misrepresentation, sign solemn undertakings and subsequently claim not to have understood them. In *Royal Bank of Scotland plc v Purvis* (1990), a wife acted as cautioner (guarantor) for money lent by R to her husband and signed a formal document accordingly. R subsequently raised an action against the wife for payment of all sums due. The wife claimed that she had signed the cautionary obligation at the request of her husband, that it had not been explained to her and that she was unfamiliar with commercial terms. She claimed that the document was void on the grounds of essential error as to its nature. Since the wife knew she was signing a document in favour of a bank which gave rise to obligations, the court could not look into what was in her mind when she signed and she was thus bound by it.

Although the courts are unwilling to overturn clear written agreements, it appears, following the case of *Smith v Bank of Scotland* (1997), that a bank is under a duty to advise a cautioner spouse to take independent advice. This appeared to bring Scots law "into line" with an English decision—*Barclays Bank plc v O'Brien* (1994)—as clear an example as one might find of courts creating new law. However, in the subsequent case of *Forsyth v Royal Bank of Scotland plc* (2000), it was accepted that the requirement of good faith, on the part of a lending bank, had been fulfilled where it had reasonable grounds to believe that the cautioner had the advantage of an advising solicitor. In *Clydesdale Bank plc v Black* (2002), good faith was held to have been satisfied where the lending bank had followed current best practice. In other words, the case of *Smith* gives guidance but is not prescriptive. Therefore, the law in this area is probably still developing.

---

5. MISREPRESENTATION

It could be said that misrepresentation is really part of error. It is fairly obvious that, in at least some of the cases considered in the previous chapter, the "misunderstanding" between the parties arose from conduct or statements of a fraudulent or careless nature. Misrepresentation arises in three distinct situations, which are partly self-explanatory: (1) innocent; (2) fraudulent and; (3) negligent. One preliminary, but very important, comment requires to be made: innocent misrepresentation does not give rise to a claim for damages. The other two forms of misrepresentation do, at least potentially.

INNOCENT MISREPRESENTATION

If a person makes a statement, honestly believing it to be true and is unaware that it is actually false, the misrepresentation counts as innocent, provided it is not actually negligent.

If the error induced by the innocent misrepresentation is essential, the contract will be void; otherwise it will be voidable. However, before a contract can be reduced on the grounds of innocent misrepresentation, the misrepresentation must have been more than merely trivial and must have been relied on by the party misled, inducing him to enter the said contract. In addition, the party wishing to reduce must be in a position to give *restitutio in integrum* (entire restoration to the original position). If this is not possible, the contract will generally have to stand.

In *Ferguson v Wilson* (1904), W, an engineer in Aberdeen, advertised for a partner to join him and invest in what he called an "established business". F replied to the advertisement and, in the course of negotiations, W was very optimistic about future business prospects. Encouraged by W's enthusiasm, F agreed to become his partner and invest in the business. F soon found that W's optimism about the state of the business had been misplaced. He raised an action to reduce the partnership agreement on the grounds of essential error, which he claimed was induced by W's fraudulent misrepresentation of the overall position of the firm. In fact, there had been no fraud but there had been innocent misrepresentation and *restitutio in integrum* was possible. The partnership agreement was set aside by the court but no damages were awarded.

However, in *Boyd & Forrest v Glasgow & South Western Railway Co.* (1912), B, contracting engineers, agreed to build a new stretch of railway track for G. The price was fixed by B at £243,000 based on data provided by G, especially particulars of test borings taken along the proposed route. B subsequently found that the information with which they had been supplied was materially inaccurate, making the work much more difficult and expensive than they had contemplated. It turned out that the original test borings, and the figures produced from them, had been the work of independent surveyors and were accurate. However, G's own engineer disagreed with some of the figures and had altered them. He had done so with the best of intentions because he honestly believed that they were inaccurate. Despite many problems, B completed the track but at a cost of £379,000, more than £100,000 above the contract price. B sued G for damages on the grounds that, having been supplied with misleading information, they had been induced to enter the contract by fraudulent misrepresentation. The House of Lords decided that there had been no fraud since G's engineer had altered the figures only because he honestly believed them to be inaccurate. If there had been any misrepresentation at all, it was innocent and thus no damages could be awarded.

FRAUDULENT MISREPRESENTATION

Like innocent misrepresentation, fraudulent misrepresentation may induce error, making the contract void or voidable. If the error is essential, the contract is void, otherwise it is voidable. "Trade puffs" or *verba jacantia* (words thrown about) are allowed some degree of latitude in practice, since few people take claims such as "good value" or "superior quality" too seriously. However, the Trade Descriptions Act 1968 provides certain criminal sanctions where there is material misdescription of goods or services. There are similar provisions regulating potentially false or misleading statements about heritable property made by solicitors, estate agents or property developers under the Property Misdescriptions Act 1991. It is not normally fraud to express a genuinely held opinion, even if it is wrong, although nowadays this could possibly give rise to an action on the grounds of negligent misrepresentation. In *Hamilton v Duke of Montrose* (1906), a statement which had been made about the capability of certain land to sustain a particular number of livestock turned out to be incorrect. There had not been any misrepresentation of fact, merely a statement of opinion. The contract was valid. A similar result can be found in *Flynn v Scott* (1949), where S sold a second-hand van to F and, in so doing, expressed an opinion that it was in good working order. Seven days later, the van broke down but F was unsuccessful in his claim that the facts had been misrepresented to him. The court accepted that S had merely expressed an opinion.

Where a statement of opinion—which turns out to be wrong—is made in the course of business and, in context, is reasonably relied on, it may count as a misrepresentation. It is more likely to be counted as negligent than fraudulent. A statement of pure future intention such as "I am hoping to expand my business over the next five years" is not a misrepresentation since, as a pure future statement, it is neither true nor false. If, however, a future statement relies on some present fact and is unreliable, it is not "pure" and may count as misrepresentation. In *British Airways Board v Taylor* (1976), an airline knowingly overbooked certain flights, but confirmed to a customer that there was a seat on a particular plane. This was held not to be a pure future statement. Even allowing for likely cancellations, the airline knew that it could not guarantee a seat.

The victim of fraud is, however, entitled to damages since fraud is a delict or civil wrong. It may also be criminal, but it need not be. At common law, the *acti quanti minoris* (very loosely meaning "something off the price") probably did not form part of Scots law. This interpretation meant that defective property could not be retained by the "innocent" party *and* the price be reduced by the damages claimed. The contract had to be cancelled and the property returned before the claim for damages could be entertained. This rule was formally abolished by the Contract (Scotland) Act 1997. In any event, the courts seemed to take a more lenient view in the case of fraud. Even before the 1997 Act, the deceived party could sue for damages even if he did not wish to reduce the contract. In *Smith v Sim* (1954), Sim advertised a public house in Montrose for sale and, through his solicitors, supplied certain figures about the turnover to Smith. Relying on these figures, Smith bought the business. He subsequently raised an action for damages claiming that the figures were fraudulent. He was entitled to proceed with his action and it was not necessary for him to rescind before doing so.

The rule of thumb that the party seeking to reduce must be able to give *restitutio in integrum* has also not been applied quite so strictly in the case of fraud. In *Spence v Crawford* (1939), S, a director of a private company, attempted to reduce a contract for the sale of shares to C, a fellow director, on the grounds of fraudulent misrepresentation. Although it was difficult for S to give exact *restitutio in integrum*, because of a change in value of the shares due to C's subsequent actions, a cash readjustment could achieve the equivalent of *restitutio*.

Misrepresentation is not fraudulent unless it was known to be untrue and conscious dishonesty must be proved. Mere carelessness is not fraud, but it may amount to negligence. *Bile Bean Manufacturing Co. v Davidson* (1906) gives a classic example of fraud. B advertised "Bile Beans" as being manufactured from secret ingredients, known only to Australian Aborigines until discovered by a famous explorer. These claims were found to be totally fictitious. D was able to claim damages for fraudulent misrepresentation.

The most famous case in this area is probably *Derry v Peek* (1889). The directors of the Plymouth, Devonport and District Tramways Company issued a share prospectus stating that the company had the right to use steam power in its trams. D bought shares in the company on the strength of that statement. In fact, the company was only entitled to use steam power if it was issued with a Board of Trade certificate. The Board declined to issue such a certificate. D failed in his action for damages against the directors of the now insolvent company since the statement had been made in the honest belief that it was true, even although the directors had not taken all reasonable care to check their statements. The law on company prospectuses was changed by statute shortly afterwards, and is now governed by the Companies Act 1985. It has been suggested that one of the effects of this case was to raise the civil burden of proof of fraud to virtually the equivalent of criminal proof.

Reference is made above to the 1912 case of *Boyd & Forrest*. In fact, the contractors were not finished with their litigation. Having lost their first action, B raised a second action—*Boyd & Forest v Glasgow & South Western Railway* (1915)—this time for reduction of the original contract on the grounds that G's innocent misrepresentation made it voidable. If B had succeeded in reducing the contract, the track could obviously not have been torn up. However, B would have been able to claim the actual cost of the railway and at least would not be making a loss. The House of Lords was not convinced that there had been any misrepresentation. Even if there had been, B's claim failed. B had not proved that the alleged misrepresentation had actually induced them to enter the contract. Furthermore, having continued to work on the track, even after discovering the inaccuracy of information, B had personally barred themselves. Finally, even if the contract was voidable, it could not be reduced, because *restitutio in integrum* was impossible.

Today, few contractors would give a fixed price on a large undertaking, such as laying a rail track. Furthermore, it is at least possible, if a similar situation did arise at the present time, that G could be sued for damages on the grounds of negligent misrepresentation.

NEGLIGENT MISREPRESENTATION

This is an area of law which, historically, has developed in more recent times and is still developing. One of the potentially confusing elements is the crossover between the law of delict and the law of contract. Negligence, *i.e.* failure in a duty of care, is a delict which can give rise to damages. There need not be any dishonesty involved and usually there is not. A representation is negligent if the person making it failed to take reasonable care in making the representation and he was under a legal duty to do so.

Hedley Byrne & Co. Ltd v Heller & Partners Ltd (1964): HB were advertising agents; they were asked by Easipower Ltd to arrange their advertising. HB enquired into the financial soundness of E by requesting their own bank to write to H&P, bankers to E. H&P stated that E were financially stable enough to honour the contract. The letter from H&P was headed "Confidential. For your private use and without responsibility on the part of this Bank". In reliance on the information contained in the letter, HB placed advertisements. Shortly afterwards, E went into liquidation, leaving HB with a substantial loss. It was clear, from subsequent enquiries, that E had been in considerable financial difficulties when H&P had made their reassuring statement. HB sued H&P for damages on the grounds of negligent misrepresentation. The case established that bankers do owe a duty of care in answering such enquiries where it is clear that recipients rely on them. However, no damages were due in this particular case because of the express provision that the information was given "without responsibility".

The above case really only dealt with the civil wrong or delictual aspects but the basic principle was extended to contractual matters in the case of *Esso Petroleum Co. v Mardon* (1976). M wished to take the tenancy of a filling station owned by EP. An experienced sales representative of EP stated that, by the third year of operation, the through-put of petrol should be around 200,000 gallons a year. M relied on this information and entered into the tenancy agreement. He did not make the profit anticipated. When EP sued him for sums due, M counterclaimed on the grounds that EP's negligent misrepresentation had induced him to enter the contract. M's counterclaim was successful; a duty of care was owed by EP.

This case was subsequently applied in two Scottish cases: *Kenway v Orcantic Ltd* (1980), where a ship did not have the carrying capacity claimed and *Foster v Craigmiller Laundry Ltd* (1980), where there was an untrue statement that a factory was free from asbestos.

By statute, it is provided, to put the matter beyond all doubt, that damages for negligent misrepresentation are recoverable in Scotland. (Law Reform (Miscellaneous Provisions)(Scotland) 1985, s.10).

SILENCE OR CONCEALMENT AS MISREPRESENTATION

When parties enter a contract, they normally do so after negotiating *at arm's length*. Neither party is going to volunteer information unless he has to. X may be negotiating to buy an article from Y for £20. X does not have to disclose to Y that he already has a third party buyer lined up who will pay £50 for it. As a general rule, contracting parties are expected to see to their own interests and satisfy themselves. This is sometimes expressed in the maxim *caveat emptor* (let the buyer beware). Although beyond the scope of this book, a buyer frequently has important statutory protection, particularly under the Sale of Goods Act 1979. What follows is basically the common law position.

If a direct question is put, it must be answered truthfully, otherwise the reply could count as fraudulent misrepresentation. Problems can arise, however, when nothing is said. Can silence count as misrepresentation? *Gillespie v Russell* (1856), a land owner, sought to cancel a lease of mineral rights he had given to R. Apparently, R had known that the land in question contained a particularly valuable seam of coal, but G had been unaware of this fact. The lease was valid as the concealment of such information by R was not fraud. He was merely seeing to his own interests. In *Royal Bank of Scotland v Greenshields* (1914), G undertook to stand caution for an individual whose bank account was overdrawn. RBS did not disclose that this customer also owed them other sums. G would not have acted as cautioner if he had known about the additional debt. G's caution was held to be valid. RBS had no duty to disclose the other debt. It has already been noted in *Smith v Bank of Scotland* (1997) and subsequent cases (see previous chapter) that, in dealing with one spouse who is standing as cautioner for the other spouse, a lending bank has certain duties to satisfy itself that the cautioner spouse has had access to independent advice.

However, there can be cases in which silence is, in fact, a subtle form of misrepresentation. *Gibson v National Cash Register Co.* (1925): G ordered two new cash registers from NCR. He was actually supplied with two second-hand machines, reconditioned to look like new. This was clearly fraudulent. Similarly in *Patterson v Landsberg & Son* (1905) (considered in Chapter 4) P, herself a dealer, bought from a London dealer certain items of jewellery which gave the clear impression of being antique. This wrong impression was not corrected by the seller.

A potentially problematic area is where parties are "economical with the truth". In fact, half-truths can be every bit as misleading as complete untruths. A second hand car dealer might truthfully tell a prospective customer that a particular car has been "thoroughly checked". But if nothing had been done to cure the many faults discovered by the check, the assurance would be worthless. In *Shankland v Robinson* (1920) the seller of a machine stated to a prospective purchaser that it was not going to be requisitioned by the government. In fact, it was requisitioned when the parties were still negotiating, but the seller failed to inform the prospective buyer—a subtle form of misrepresentation.

CONTRACTS NOT SUBJECT TO "ARM'S LENGTH" RULE

Having established the general "arm's length" rule, there may be occasions where parties to a contract *do* require to make full disclosure to one another. In other words, they do not merely contract at arm's length. Contracts which are not subject to the arm's length rule fall into two main categories:

Contracts *uberrimae fidei* (of utmost good faith)

These are contracts of so-called utmost good faith, insurance or partnership being the two generally accepted categories. This is no mere academic matter. In all insurance contracts, the policy will be voidable if the party insured has failed to disclose some material fact which might affect the risk being undertaken by the insurer, even if the insurer did not ask a specific question relating to it. This is powerfully illustrated by the case of *The Spathari* (1925). D, a Greek ship broker, resident in Glasgow, bought the SS Spathari, a Finnish ship at Hull, with the intention of selling her to a syndicate of Greeks at Samos. At the time, Greek vessels had great difficulty in getting insurance due to poor safety records. D came to an arrangement with B, a Glasgow ship broker, that the ship would be transferred into B's name, that the latter would register and insure her, ostensibly as owner, until the voyage to Samos was complete. On the voyage to Greece, the Spathari sank. The insurance company was entitled to refuse payment on account of B's failure to disclose a material fact, namely the "Greek" element of the boat, even though that element might appear somewhat tenuous.

Contracts involving a fiduciary relationship

These are contracts where the parties stand in a relationship of trust to one another, *e.g.* parent and child, agent and principal, solicitor and client. Common sense would indicate that such parties do not normally contract with each other as strangers. Solicitors have strict professional rules about making contracts with clients outwith the provision of normal professional services. *McPherson's Trustees v Watt* (1877): W, an Advocate in Aberdeen, arranged for a trust, to which he was solicitor, to sell four houses to his brother. W did not disclose that his brother had already agreed to resell him two of the houses at a favourable price. W should have made full disclosure to the trust about the true nature of the transaction. The contract of sale was void.

OTHER FACTORS AFFECTING VALIDITY

In the following cases, the validity of the contract is affected, as the consent of one of the parties has been improperly obtained.

Facility and circumvention

A contract can be reduced where the party misled is not insane, but is suffering from weakness of mind due to old age or ill health, *i.e.* there is a "facility". Circumvention is the motive to mislead, but falls short of actual fraud. If both factors are present and the party misled suffers some kind of harm or loss as a result of the contract, it is voidable. A classic and somewhat melodramatic case is *Cairns v Marianski* (1850), where F, an elderly man, living with a daughter and son-in-law M, transferred property to the son-in-law. After F's death, C, his other daughter, successfully had the transfer documents reduced. There was evidence that F had been under the "command and control" of M. Similarly, in *MacGilvray v Gilmartin* (1986), M, the executor of his late mother's estate, successfully raised an action to reduce a deed which she had signed transferring heritable property to his sister. When she signed the deed, the mother was severely depressed, due to the death of her husband and the daughter had taken advantage of this situation.

Undue influence

A contract is voidable if one person is in a position to influence another and abuses this position to induce this other party to make the contract to his disadvantage. It is most likely to occur in fiduciary relationships, such as parent and child, doctor and patient, solicitor and client— but it could take place in any relationship where there is an element of confidence. There is no need, however, to prove that the weaker party was subject to any facility. In *Gray v Binny* (1879) a father left an estate to his son by will. His mother persuaded the son—with the help of the family solicitor to whom she owed money—to transfer the estate to her. The transfer was subsequently reduced. The mother and the solicitor had taken advantage of the son's ignorance as to his rights and of the fact that he had confidence in them.

Force and fear

Generally, if a contract is entered into because of force or fear, it is void through lack of true consent. The threats may be physical or mental, *e.g.* "blackmail", and could be made in respect of a near relative as well as to the victim himself. In *Gow v Henry* (1899) a threat to dismiss a workman from his post, without just cause, counted as force and fear. However, a threat to do something legal, such as pursuing a legitimate debt, or asking a dishonest employee to resign rather than call in the police, is not force and fear. In the very old case of *Earl of Orkney v Vinfra* (1606), the Earl commanded V to sign a contract. V refused, but then did so when the Earl threatened to kill him. The contract was void. In *Hunter v Bradford Trust*

Ltd (1977), two sisters in financially embarrassed circumstances came to an arrangement with a property company over the sale by roup of certain heritable property. On the night before the roup, a director of the company discovered that the signed agreement did not reflect what he thought the terms of the contract were. He refused to proceed with the sale until the sisters signed a new agreement. After prolonged discussion well into the night, the sisters signed the new agreement which was less favourable to them than the first. They were not successful in their attempt to have the second agreement reduced. In *Hislop v Dickson Motors (Forres) Ltd* (1978), a cashier was accused by her employers of embezzling certain funds. She admitted the accusation and agreed to try to repay the money. She voluntarily handed over her car and a blank bank deposit account withdrawal form. The employer subsequently discovered that she also had a current account. Two representatives of the employing company went to her house and after heated words, she gave them a blank signed cheque, with which they withdrew the current account balance. At her trial, the charge against the cashier was "not proven". In a subsequent civil action, she was unsuccessful in attempting to have the delivery of the car and the deposit account withdrawal form set aside. However, the signature on the blank cheque was set aside on the grounds that her consent had been vitiated by force and fear.

Extortion

The general rule is that a contract is neither void nor voidable merely on the grounds of being a poor bargain. Parties normally contract at arms length and should look to their own interests. In *McLachlan v Watson* (1874), M took a 10 year lease of a Glasgow hotel under an arrangement which could not, by any standards, have been considered to be other than a poor bargain and which included payment of an annual "bonus" of £600 to W. M died four years into the lease but his widow was unsuccessful in her attempts to have the lease reduced. It is different if the contract is induced by fraudulent misrepresentation or if there are other vitiating factors. However, under the Consumer Credit Act 1974, the court has power to re-open and alter or set aside, *any* credit agreement if the rate of interest appears to be extortionate, *i.e.* if it grossly contravenes ordinary fair dealings. No set rate of interest is laid down as being extortionate. Factors which the court would take into account are interest rates, the age of the debtor, his/her experience, business capacity and state of health; also the degree of risk undertaken by the creditor and the relationship between the parties. This provision is not restricted to consumer credit agreements as defined by the Act nor is it subject to any financial limit.

SUMMARY OF THE EFFECT OF VITIATING FACTORS

Error
(1)   of law—no effect on the contract;
(2)   in transmission—no contract;

(3)   of expression—reduction at common law or statutory rectification;
(4)   of intention:
    (a)   unilateral—contract valid;
    (b)   common—contract void, but only if error is essential and refers to facts, not merely opinion;
    (c)   mutual—contract valid if error is collateral, but void if essential.

Misrepresentation

(1)   Fraudulent and negligent—contract voidable if misrepresentation is collateral and void if the misrepresentation is essential; damages in either case, but in delict rather than contract. Contract cannot generally be set aside if third parties have acquired rights in good faith and for value, if *restitutio in integrum* is not possible or if personal bar has operated.
(2)   Innocent—as above, but no damages.

Force and fear
Contract void.

Facility and circumvention and undue influence
Contract voidable.

[The above summary is reproduced from David Field and Alasdair Gordon, *Elements of Scots Law* (2nd ed., W. Green/Sweet & Maxwell, Edinburgh, 1997).]

---

6. ILLEGAL AGREEMENTS

A contract must be lawful both in its objects and in the way in which it is performed. If either of these elements is not satisfied, the courts will not enforce the agreement. Such agreements are known as *pacta illicita* (illegal agreements), although that title is somewhat misleading. It would not necessarily be illegal, in the sense of being criminal, to set up such agreements, but the court would not enforce them nor would it award damages in the event of breach. Some of these agreements would more properly be called unenforceable. The general principle is *ex turpi causa non oritur actio* (no action arises out of an immoral situation) and it is the duty of the judge to take notice that it is an illegal agreement.

In *Hamilton v Main* (1823), H sought to set aside a promissory note for £60 which he had granted to M in payment of an account for his stay at M's public house for a seven day period. During that period, H had, in company with a prostitute, consumed a vast quantity of wines and spirits in a drunken orgy. The promissory note was unenforceable in law.

Another maxim in this area of law is *in turpi causa melior est conditio possidentis* (in an immoral situation, the position of the possessor is the better one). Thus, the loss is allowed to lie where it falls, *e.g.* a person pays money for an illegal drug, which is then not supplied. He will not be able to take legal steps to recover the money from the drug dealer. In *Barr v Crawford* (1983), a woman was informed that the chances of her taking over the licence of a public house from her late husband were not good. She paid out over £10,000 in bribes in an attempt to secure the transfer. She later sought to recover the bribe money, but her action was dismissed.

However, when the parties are not *in pari delicto* (equally at fault), the court may assist the party who is less blameworthy. In the English case of *Strongman v Sincock* (1955), architects had promised builders that they would obtain necessary building licences. They failed to do so which made the completed building illegal. The builders were successful in their claim for damages against the architects.

STATUTORY ILLEGALITY

An Act of Parliament can place a limit on the freedom of a person to make a contract. Sometimes it may even declare a certain type of contract to be illegal. Such a contract would be null and void. However, the courts may give effect to rights which are incidental to the contract, to prevent one party from gaining an unfair advantage over another. In *Cuthbertson v Lowes* (1870), C sold L two fields of potatoes at £24 per Scots acre. Under the Weights and Measures Acts, this contract was void, as imperial measure had become obligatory. L took delivery of the potatoes, but did not pay the full price. C sued for the balance. Even though the contract could not be enforced by the court, C was entitled to the market value of the potatoes at the time of harvesting. By contrast, in *Jamieson v Watt's Trustee* (1950), W requested J, a joiner, to carry out certain work. Under the Defence Regulations 1939, this required a licence. J applied for a licence to carry out work valued at £40, knowing that the total cost would be higher. When he tendered an account of over £114, he was not entitled to claim the amount in excess of the licence figure.

In Chapter 7, it will be demonstrated that it is illegal for parties to attempt to contract out of certain provisions of the Unfair Contract Terms Act 1977. Various forms of discrimination on the grounds of gender, race and disability are also prohibited by statute.

ILLEGALITY AT COMMON LAW

A contract is illegal at common law, if its purpose is criminal, *e.g.* to commit a murder; fraudulent, *e.g.* to swindle a third party; or immoral. In *Pearce v Brooks* (1886), a firm of coach builders agreed to hire out a specially constructed brougham carriage to a prostitute. The firm knew that she intended to use the carriage to ply her trade around the streets of London. She failed to pay the carriage hire, but the sum could not be recovered in court as the purpose of the contract was immoral. There is a fourth area of illegality at common law—agreements contrary to public policy—which are now separately considered.

AGREEMENTS CONTRARY TO PUBLIC POLICY

Public policy, like public morality, is notoriously difficult to define, particularly in a complex modern society. However, some agreements are clearly against public policy, *e.g.* contracting with an enemy alien or interfering with the administration of justice. Less easy, are contracts which seek to restrict a person's freedom to work or to trade, *i.e.* contracts in restraint of trade, although these are mainly governed now by the Competition Act 1998 (see below).

Closely related (and the titles are used almost interchangeably) are restrictive covenants, which are governed by common law. A restrictive covenant seeks to restrict a person's freedom to work where he pleases, for whom he pleases and in what line of business he pleases.

The very general common law rule is that contracts in restraint of trade or restrictive covenants are void—unless it can be shown that the restrictions are reasonable both for the parties to the contract and for the public. The courts will also want to be convinced that the parties are contracting on equal terms.

In *Schroeder Music Publishing v Macaulay* (1974), M, a young songwriter, had a contract with S giving the latter exclusive rights to his compositions for five years. S could renew this contract for a further five years, or could end it at any time. They were under no obligation to publish any songs and M had no right to terminate the contract. When M became better known, he successfully sought release from the contract.

Agreements between employers and employees

A restrictive covenant seeks to prevent an employee from working in competition with his former employer in the future. This may be part of the employee's contract of employment and normally will only take effect when, for whatever reason, the employment comes to an end. Even if the employee is wrongfully dismissed, the restrictive covenant may still apply. The covenants are probably most common in service industries or in businesses where there are trade secrets or sensitive information.

The courts do not generally take kindly to an individual being unreasonably restrained and such an agreement will not be enforced unless the employer can show that he is protecting his legitimate interests. It is legitimate for an employer to protect his trade secrets or his customer base. However, it is not legitimate to prevent fair competition.

If the courts are asked to uphold a restrictive covenant, it will, in any event, have to pass the reasonableness test. Thus, the courts will also look at all the factors involved, *e.g.* the type of business, radius or customer area, location (*e.g.* city, large town, small town or rural area) and the status of the employee within the business. The courts tend to interpret "reasonable" more strictly in the relationship of employer and employee, than between buyer and seller of a business. There is a large body of case law in this area, of which only a sample can be given.

In *Mason v Provident Clothing & Supply Co Ltd* (1913), M was employed as a salesman with P. The company had branches all over England, but M was employed only in a limited area of London. He had agreed, when he first took up employment with P, that he would not become employed in a similar business within a radius of 25 miles of London and within a period of three years. As M was employed in a relatively minor capacity and, considering the dense population of London, the restraint was far wider than reasonably necessary and was unenforceable. By contrast, in *The Scottish Farmers' Dairy Co. (Glasgow) Ltd v McGhee* (1933), a milkman was unable to overturn a restriction placed on him not to sell milk within one mile of his former employer's place of business. The court took account of the fact that a regular milkman transferring his allegiance to another employer in the same area was almost bound to take a significant number of his former employer's customers with him. In *Rentokil Ltd v Kramer* (1986), K's former employers were able to prevent him from canvassing clients from R for a period of two years after leaving.

Fitch v Dewes (1921): F was employed as managing clerk to D, a solicitor. F had started his employment as a junior clerk and, over a period of years, had worked his way up and had come to know, and be known, by D's clients. At the outset, F had agreed that if he should ever terminate his employment, he would not become engaged in the business of a solicitor (either on his own account or working for anyone else) within a radius of seven miles of D's office. This restriction was reasonable and enforceable. D had done no more than attempt to prevent his clients being enticed away from him, which he was legally entitled to do. On the other hand, in *Dallas McMillan & Sinclair v Simpson* (1989), the court refused to prevent an outgoing partner of a firm of Glasgow solicitors from practising within 20 miles of Glasgow Cross. It need scarcely be said that the radius in the latter case covers a significant percentage of the urban population of Scotland. In an older case of *Stewart v Stewart* (1899), a radius of 20 miles from Elgin imposed by a photographer on his assistant (who was also his brother) was held to be reasonable and enforceable—but that restriction applied to a thinly populated area of Scotland.

An important factor is the right, referred to above, of an employer to protect his trade secrets. A classic modern example is *Bluebell Apparel v Dickinson* (1980). D was taken on as a management trainee by B, manufacturers of "Wrangler" jeans. Within a few months, D was in sole charge of one of B's Scottish factories. Shortly afterwards, he intimated that he was leaving to take up a position with a rival jeans manufacturer, Levi Strauss. Both companies operate on a world wide basis. B were entitled to interdict D from continuing in employment with Levi Strauss, as he was in possession of trade secrets which would be of value to a business competitor. The two-year and world wide restriction in his original contract was reasonable, in the circumstances.

A trade secret need not necessarily refer to a secret technical process. It could refer to any confidential information and would have to be a matter of proof in particular circumstances. In *TSB Bank plc v Connell* (1997), the business of a bank—including the identities of customers, their banking arrangements and their family and financial circumstances—was included in this category.

The courts do not have power to change an agreement into which parties have voluntarily entered. Either the agreement stands or it falls. Anyone thus seeking to impose a restrictive covenant ought to bear this in mind. If the restrictive covenant is set aside by the court, it falls entirely and leaves no protection for the party who originally imposed it. *Empire Meat Co v Patrick* (1939): P was manager of a butcher's shop. He was well known to the regular customers who came mainly from within a one-mile radius of the shop. On first taking up his employment, P had agreed that he would not set up business nor work for another butcher within a five-mile radius of his employer's premises. This restriction was too great and thus entirely unenforceable. A one-mile radius would have been acceptable but the court had no power to change the agreement.

There is yet a further complication. What if there are, say, two parts to the agreement, one of which seems reasonable and the other does not? Does the entire agreement fall? Provided the two parts are severable, *i.e.* capable of being separated and standing on their own, the court may be prepared to allow one part to stand but to delete ("blue pencil") the other part. However, as explained above, the court will not substitute a reasonable restriction for an unreasonable one. *Mulvein v Murray* (1908): Mulvein owned a footwear business, employing Murray as a travelling salesman. Murray had signed an agreement that he would not: (1) sell to or canvas any of Mulvein's customers nor; (2) sell or travel in any of the towns or districts traded in by Mulvein, for one year after leaving his employment. The first provision was reasonable but the second provision was not. The reasonable part of the restriction was severable (*i.e.* it could stand on its own) and thus enforceable. The other restriction was void.

AGREEMENTS BETWEEN BUYER AND SELLER OF A BUSINESS

When a purchaser buys the goodwill of a business, he will usually insist that the seller binds himself not to set up in competition within a certain area and/or time. The courts are more willing in these cases to enforce the agreement, but the test of reasonableness will still apply. The agreements must not cover a longer period of time, nor a wider area of operations, than is necessary. A famous case is *Nordenfelt v Maxim Nordenfelt Guns and Ammunition Co. Ltd* (1894). N, the owner of a cannon manufacturing business sold it to M and agreed not to engage in the making of cannon anywhere in the world for 25 years. As the business was quite unique and customers so few—namely governments—the restriction, considering all the facts and circumstances of the case, was not too wide nor contrary to the public interest. By contrast, in *Dumbarton Steamboat Co. Ltd v*

MacFarlane (1899), MacF was a partner in a carrier's business, which traded in the Glasgow area. The business was sold to D, who insisted that MacF agree not to carry on a similar business anywhere in the United Kingdom for a period of 10 years. A restriction affecting the entire United Kingdom was too wide, since D's area of operation was restricted to Glasgow and the West of Scotland. As in the case of employers and employees, the court had no power to vary or rewrite the agreement. These two cases demonstrate that the question is very much one of degree and circumstances in each instance.

JOINT AGREEMENTS BETWEEN MANUFACTURERS OR TRADERS

These types of agreement, although not unknown in common law, are mainly regulated by statute and delegated legislation to protect the interests of the public. Until relatively recently, cartels were perfectly legal and not uncommon in business. More mature persons (including the writer of this book) also remember resale price maintenance, when the prices of the same goods in all shops were identical. The manufacturer or wholesaler only supplied traders with goods on the condition that these same goods would be retailed at a certain price. Most of these restrictive practices were swept away by the Resale Prices Act 1964, subsequently replaced by the Resale Prices Act 1976. Other landmark legislation of the same year was the Restrictive Court Act and the Restrictive Trade Practices Act.

Considerable water has since flowed under the legal bridge and the above legislation has come and gone. The current law is found in the Competition Act 1998 and Articles 81 and 82 of the EC Treaty. Competition law is a subject in its own right and only a few basic comments can be included in this book. The 1998 Act introduced a requirement to interpret its provisions in the light of the competition law of the European Community. The Act covers, for example, agreements which fix buying or selling prices, limit production, markets or investment or which share markets or sources of supply. There is provision for exemption. The Act also set up the Competition Commission, taking the place of the former Monopolies and Mergers Commission.

SOLUS AGREEMENTS

These are agreements between the supplier of goods and the distributor or retailer under which the retailer sells only one brand of goods, in return for which he receives special discounts or privileges. Such *solus* (alone, only) agreements are quite common but, if challenged, must again meet the reasonableness test. The relative bargaining position of the parties might also be taken into account. In *Petrofina (G.B.) v Martin* (1966), M purchased a garage, which was the subject of a *solus* agreement with P. M made new arrangements with P to the effect that, in return for rebates, he would supply only P's petrol and oil. The agreement was to last for 12 years or until such time as M had sold 600,000 gallons of petrol, whichever was the longer period. M discovered that he was trading at a loss and, as a result, formed a limited company and came to an arrangement with Esso. P tried to enforce the original agreement but it was found to be unreasonable and invalid for a number of reasons, two of them being: (1) the 12-year period was too long and (2) the restriction obliged him to carry on his business, even though it was running at a loss. As in other restrictive agreements, there is the possibility of more than one restriction being imposed. If these are severable (as explained above) the court may uphold one restriction and reject the other. In *Esso Petroleum Co. Ltd v Harpers Garages (Stourport) Ltd* (1968), a 21-year *solus* agreement in respect of one filling station was set aside, whereas another agreement for four-and-a-half years between the same parties— but in respect of a different filling station—was upheld.

---

7. EXCLUSION CLAUSES IN CONTRACTS

At an early stage in this book it was emphasised that, before anyone can claim that a contract—and, thus, a binding obligation—exists, there must be *consensus in idem*. This means that both parties are in one mind, as to the essential elements which make up the main terms and conditions of the obligation, from the outset.

Sometimes, one of the two parties may have greater bargaining power than the other and will try to bring conditions into the contract of which the other party has no knowledge—or, if he does know about them, does not quite understand or realise their significance. The party with the greater bargaining power might attempt to incorporate an exclusion (of liability) or an exemption in his own favour by, say, printing appropriate wording on a "ticket" or placing it on a notice or similar display, *e.g.*:

PERSONS ENTER THESE PREMISES AT THEIR OWN RISK

THE MANAGEMENT ACCEPTS NO RESPONSIBILITY FOR ARTICLES LEFT IN THIS CLOAKROOM

IN THE EVENT OF ANY DAMAGE OCCURRING TO THIS ITEM WHEN IN CONTROL OF THE COMPANY, LIABILITY SHALL BE RESTRICTED TO £100 PER ITEM

When a ticket is issued, it can be intended either as a receipt for money paid or it may be a voucher to claim property or services, *e.g.* uplifting goods from a dry cleaner or handing over a cinema ticket. Quite often, the ticket will have conditions printed on it, or it may refer to conditions published elsewhere. Sometimes there will be no ticket, but a notice may be displayed on business premises which is intended to be a written exclusion clause in an otherwise unwritten contract. Sometimes the clause will appear both on a ticket and on a notice.

As the name would suggest, the purpose of such a clause is to exclude or limit liability, particularly for negligence. Whether or not such a clause is part of the contract depends partly on the nature of the ticket or notice and partly on the question of whether the other party's attention has been properly drawn to it.

ATTEMPTS TO IMPOSE POST-FORMATION CONDITIONS

One thing is quite clear: additional conditions cannot be added after the contract has been formed, unless there is the consent of both parties. In *Olley v Marlborough Court Ltd* (1949), Mr and Mrs O made a hotel booking. On the wall of their room was a notice *"THE PROPRIETORS WILL NOT HOLD THEMSELVES RESPONSIBLE FOR ARTICLES LOST AND STOLEN"*. Mrs O left her fur coat in the room, locked the door and gave the key to the hotel receptionist. A thief obtained the key and stole the coat. The hotel company unsuccessfully attempted to rely on the notice on the wall to exclude them from liability. They could not do so, since the condition was not known to Mr and Mrs O until after the contract had been formed and was not part of it. *Thornton v Shoe Lane Parking Ltd* (1971): T drove his car into an automatic car park. He could only gain entry by taking a ticket from a machine. Inside the car park was a notice showing the charges and excluding liability for damage to cars or for personal injury. The ticket issued by the machine showed the date and time of arrival and referred to "conditions". T was injured as he left the car park. The court was clear that the contract was formed when T took the ticket from the machine. Accordingly, the additional conditions had not been communicated to him at that time and were not contractually binding.

THE NATURE OF THE TICKET

For a condition printed on a ticket to be essential to, or an integral part of, the contract, the ticket itself must be *more* than just a voucher or receipt. It will usually be recognised that a ticket is an integral part of contracts of carriage (*e.g.* a train journey) or deposit (*e.g.* left luggage) and the courts would expect a reasonable person to be aware that such contracts are normally subject to published conditions.

If the ticket is not an integral part of the contract and is merely a receipt or voucher, conditions printed on it will not generally be binding. In *Chapelton v Barry Urban District Council* (1940), conditions excluding liability were not binding on a man who had hired a deck chair on the beach and had been injured as a result of using it. The ticket was, in the circumstances of the case, taken to be only a receipt and words printed on it were not part of the contract. *Taylor v Glasgow Corporation* (1952): T went to a public baths for a hot bath. She paid at the entrance kiosk and received a ticket, which she had to hand over to the attendant as a voucher. On the front of the ticket were the words *"FOR CONDITIONS SEE OTHER SIDE"*. On the back were words excluding G from liability for any damage to property or personal injuries. T knew that there was printing on the back of the ticket but did not read it. T alleged that, due to the negligence of a bath attendant, she was allowed to fall down some stairs, causing her injury. She sued G for damages. G unsuccessfully attempted to rely on the exclusion clause on the back of the ticket. The ticket was merely a voucher or receipt to show what service T had paid for and to give entry to the appropriate part of the baths. The exclusion clause was not part of the contract.

Sometimes, even though no notice is given of a specific exclusion, a person may still be bound by it because he is aware of it due to previous dealings between the parties. However, before allowing this, the courts would have to be convinced that the previous dealings had been consistent. *McCutcheon v David MacBrayne Ltd* (1964) 28: McC sought damages in respect of his car which had been lost when MacB's ferryboat sank on a trip from Islay to Tarbert. His brother-in-law, McS, had arranged the shipment of the car. Both men had, in the past, sent items by MacB's ferry. In principle, MacB required shippers to sign a so-called "risk note" which excluded MacB from certain liabilities. In previous dealings, both McC and McS sometimes had, and sometimes had not, signed such notes. In the case of the present contract, only a receipt had been issued to McS and no risk note had been signed by him. The wording of the exclusion clause contained in risk notes was also published in MacB's office and on Islay pier. The court was not convinced that there had been a consistent course, as risk notes had sometimes been signed and sometimes not. Thus the clause was not part of the contract in question and McC was entitled to compensation for his lost car.

WAS ATTENTION ADEQUATELY DRAWN TO THE CONDITION?

Even if the ticket is integral to the contract (*i.e.* more than a mere ticket or voucher), the existence of conditions must still be adequately brought to the attention of the customer. If the conditions are not adequately drawn to his attention, the contract itself is still valid but the conditions on the ticket are not binding. In *Henderson v Stevenson* (1875), S bought a ticket for a voyage from Dublin to Whitehaven. On the back of the ticket was printed: *"THE COMPANY INCUR NO LIABILITY WHATEVER IN RESPECT OF LOSS, INJURY, OR DELAY TO THE PASSENGER OR TO HIS OR HER LUGGAGE, WHETHER ARISING FROM THE ACT, NEGLECT, OR DEFAULT OF THEIR SERVANTS OR OTHERWISE"*. S did not read this condition and the clerk who issued the ticket did not draw his attention to it. The steamer was wrecked off the Isle of Man due to the negligence of the company's servants. S's claim for damages was successful. The condition had not been imported into the contract of carriage. There was no reference on the front of the ticket to the condition on the back. S's attention had not been adequately brought to the condition and he was not bound by it. *Williamson v North of Scotland Navigation Co* (1916): conditions had been printed on the front of a steamer ticket but in the smallest typeface known. These conditions had not been validly incorporated into the contract. By contrast, in *Hood v Anchor Line* (1918), operators of a shipping line successfully incorporated an exclusion clause into a contract when it was handed to a passenger in an envelope clearly asking passengers to read the information on the enclosed ticket. The exclusion clause was printed legibly on the front of the ticket.

EXCLUSIONS AT ARM'S LENGTH

If parties who are both in business elect to sign contracts at arm's length, they will be bound by them—subject to "standard form" contracts requiring to be fair and reasonable under the Unfair Contract Terms Act 1977, considered further below. In *Photo Production Ltd v Securicor Transport Ltd* (1980), S agreed to provide security inspection at a factory. One of their employees criminally started a fire in the factory, resulting in a loss of £615,000. The factory owners sued for damages. S relied on a clause in its standard conditions which excluded liability in most situations. The clause clearly covered acts such as that of S's employee; S were not liable. *Ailsa Craig Fishing Co. v Malvern Fishing Co.* (1982): two fishing boats were tied up in Aberdeen harbour. When the tide rose, the bow of one of the boats caught under the quay and she sank, sinking another boat in the process. S had been engaged to patrol the harbour to check on safety and security. S relied on a clause in their contract limiting liability to £1,000 for any one claim and £10,000 for total claims for any one accident. The limitation was held to be effective. The parties had signed a contract at arm's length.

SIGNING A TICKET

It would seem that if a person actually signs a ticket, he is presumed to have read and accepted the conditions (unless misrepresentation took place). Being asked to sign in this way is not common but it can still happen occasionally, *e.g.* at a dry cleaners, if the material of items taken in for cleaning cannot be identified by its label. (See *Curtis v Chemical Cleaning and Dyeing Co.* (1951), below.)

SUMMARY OF EXCLUSIONS THROUGH TICKETS

(1) An exclusion clause cannot usually be brought in through the use of a ticket if it is only a voucher or receipt. In contracts of carriage or deposit, parties normally understand that the contract will be subject to certain published conditions.

(2) If it is more than a mere voucher or receipt, and the person knew that there were conditions but did not read them, he will still be bound by them if they are of the type expected in that kind of contract—subject to the Unfair Contract Terms Act 1977 ("UCTA").

(3) If the person has actually read the conditions, he will be bound by them (subject to UCTA).

(4) If he did not know of the conditions, he will only be bound by them (subject to UCTA) if they have been properly brought to his attention. In the light of decided cases, that seems to mean that either the conditions must be clearly printed on the front of the ticket or, if the actual conditions are to be found somewhere else, there must be a clear reference on the front of the ticket that this is the case.

UNFAIR CONTRACT TERMS ACT 1977

The title of this Act is somewhat misleading as it does not actually cover all unfair contract terms—only exclusion clauses. Under UCTA, certain exclusion clauses are declared void whereas others are subject to a test of whether they are "fair and reasonable". UCTA only applies to attempts to exclude liability by businesses. In this situation, "business" includes companies, partnerships, sole traders, professionals, local authorities and government departments. It does not include individuals who act in a personal or private capacity.

Part I of UCTA applies to England and Wales, Part II to Scotland and Part III to all of the UK. The Act applies to the following types of contracts.

Contracts in the course of a business
Consumer contracts: where one of the parties deals in the course of a business and the other does not and the goods are of a type normally bought by a consumer.
Standard form contracts: the contract is only offered, or accepted, on the basis of the party's "standard" conditions. These, in fact, are often consumer contracts but a contract between two businesses can be brought into the provisions of the Act where it is "standard form" (see further below).

Contracts for the sale of goods
This includes goods bought under credit or hire purchase agreements.

Contracts for the hire of goods
This would include moveable items such as a car or television set, but not a lease of heritable property.

Contracts of employment
This also includes contracts of apprenticeship.

Contracts for services

This covers a wide area including services provided by a law agent, accountant, builder, dry-cleaner, car-park owner, bus company, left luggage.

Contracts allowing entry to someone's property

Included are items such as a ticket for admission to a sports ground, cinema, safari park, museum, swimming pool. Also included, are parties who are given permission to enter property *e.g.* to carry out repairs.

Certain contracts are, however, excluded from the Act. These include insurance and contracts for the transfer of an interest in land. A condition in a contract to which UCTA applies is void if it relates to exclusion of liability for death or personal injury. The condition is of no effect in other cases unless it was fair and reasonable when the contract was made. The contract itself is not voided; only the purported exclusion.

The burden of proving that a term is fair and reasonable lies with the party who is seeking to rely on it, *i.e.* that party will always be a business. Very simple examples of the types of clause regularly encountered are:

NO REFUNDS WILL BE GIVEN UNLESS ACCOMPANIED BY A RECEIPT

ANY CLAIM RELATING TO THIS CONTRACT MUST BE MADE WITHIN FOURTEEN DAYS

ALL PHOTOGRAPHIC MATERIAL IS ACCEPTED ON THE BASIS THAT ITS VALUE DOES NOT EXCEED THE COST OF THE MATERIAL ITSELF

THE BUYER'S CLAIM SHALL BE RESTRICTED TO DAMAGES; HE SHALL NOT BE ENTITLED TO SUE FOR DELIVERY

When considering whether such a condition is valid, the court must apply a test of reasonableness. The condition will be valid if it was fair and reasonable at the outset for it to be included, having regard to the circumstances known to the parties at the time the contract was made.

In contracts for the supply of goods, the court must also take account of circumstances such as the relative bargaining strengths of the parties—and whether the customer knew, or ought to have known, of the condition and its effect. If the condition limits liability to a fixed sum, the court will take account of the trader's financial resources and will consider the extent to which he could have covered himself by insurance.

Nowadays most businesses, which provide services, take out insurance cover to protect themselves against the risks to which they are subject.

SUMMARY OF MAIN POINTS OF UCTA

(1) It relates only to contracts "in the course of a business" as defined, i.e. consumer or standard form contracts, and not to transactions between private parties;

(2) Liability for death or personal injury caused by negligence cannot be excluded;

(3) Other exclusions must pass the "reasonableness" test;

(4) The burden of proof is on the party inserting the exclusion to show that it is fair and reasonable in the particular circumstances of the case.

UNFAIR TERMS IN CONSUMER CONTRACTS REGULATIONS 1999

The above Regulations (SI 1999/2083) came into effect on October 1, 1999 and were subsequently amended (SI 2001/1186). They replaced Regulations of the same title dated 1994. A consumer (a natural person acting outside his trade, business or profession) can avoid a term in a contract for goods or services by showing that it is unfair, contrary to good faith or causes imbalance to his detriment. This goes further than UCTA which only deals with exclusions of liability. The Regulations retain the obligation on the Director General of Fair Trading to take action, if necessary through the courts, to prevent the use of terms which he considers unfair. The 1999 Regulations give a further list of qualifying bodies who may also, in appropriate circumstances, apply to the court to prevent the continued use of an unfair contract term. As a result of the 2001 amendments, the Financial Services Authority is added to the list.

The basic premise that parties are free to contract at arm's length is not affected. Thus if parties individually negotiate the selling price of a particular item at arm's length, the Regulations do not apply. However, they do apply to standard term contracts and to contracts of insurance.

ADDITIONAL CASES FOR STUDY OR DISCUSSION

In *L'Estrange v Graucob* (1934), L'E bought—for use in her café—a coin-operated cigarette machine from G, and signed a purchase agreement containing certain conditions in small print. These conditions exempted G from liability if the machine did not work. As L'E had signed the agreement, she was bound by it. She had failed to read the exclusions properly but they had not been misrepresented to her nor concealed from her. (If this case came up today, it would be covered by UCTA.)

Curtis v Chemical Cleaning & Dyeing Co. Ltd (1951): C took a wedding dress to the cleaners and was asked to sign a receipt containing conditions. The assistant stated that, under the conditions, the company would not accept liability for damage to the sequins on the dress. The dress, in fact, was returned badly stained. The company pleaded the exemption clause on the receipt which, in fact, excluded them from all liability for damage to cleaned goods. The company was not able rely on this clause as its effect had been misrepresented, albeit innocently, to C by the assistant.

Interfoto Picture Library Ltd v Stiletto Visual Programmes Ltd (1988): S, an advertising agency required period photos of the 1950s. On March 5, 1984, S telephoned IPL, a commercial photographic library, to enquire if it had anything suitable. The same day, IPL dispatched 47 transparencies, packed in a jiffy bag, with a delivery note. At the top right hand corner of the note, the date of return was clearly stated as March 19, 1984. At the foot of the document under the heading of "Conditions" there were nine conditions in four columns. Condition 2 read *"All transparencies must be returned to us within fourteen days from the date of delivery. A holding fee of £5 plus VAT will be charged for each transparency retained by you longer than the said period of fourteen days"*. S did not actually use the transparencies and forgot about them. They were not returned until April 2, 1984. An invoice then followed for holding charges of £3,783.50. The court dismissed this claim, although it awarded a *quantum meruit* payment. Where a condition in a contract is particularly onerous or unusual and would not be generally known to the other party, the party seeking to enforce must show that it has been fairly and reasonably brought to the attention of the other party. This case was followed in Scotland in *Montgomery Litho Ltd v Maxwell* (2000).

In *Woodman v Photo Trade Processing* (1981) (unreported),W, an experienced amateur photographer, took wedding pictures for some friends and gave the exposed film for processing to his local branch of Dixons. When he called to pick up the film, he found that part of it was missing, as were the prints of the missing section. These items were never found. Dixons were very apologetic but pointed out that there was an exclusion clause displayed in the shop saying *"ALL PHOTOGRAPHIC MATERIALS ARE ACCEPTED ON THE BASIS THAT THEIR VALUE DOES NOT EXCEED THE COST OF THE MATERIAL ITSELF"*. Dixons offered him a free replacement film. In an English County Court judgement, it was held that the exclusion clause was not fair and reasonable and thus fell within the provisions of UCTA. W was awarded £75 in damages.

Smith v Eric Bush (1989): a valuer was instructed by a building society to carry out a mortgage valuation on a house. The valuation was negligently carried out, as the surveyor noticed that chimney breasts had been removed in a downstairs room but did not check whether the brickwork above had also been removed or was properly supported. No such steps had been taken and this fact should have been obvious to a professional surveyor. The unsupported chimney later collapsed into the main upstairs bedroom. The contract for valuation was actually between the building society and the surveyors, although the borrower was obliged to pay the fee. The mortgage application form and the valuation report contained a disclaimer of liability for the accuracy of the report covering both the building society and the surveyors. The borrower was also informed that the report was not a structural survey and she was advised to obtain independent professional advice. According to normal practice, the building society provided her with a copy of the report, which stated that no essential repairs were necessary, and she relied on it. The surveyors did owe the borrower a duty of care, as it was clearly foreseeable that she would rely on the report. The terms of the disclaimer which the borrower had been asked to sign fell within the provisions of UCTA and were unreasonable. This English case was not followed in Scotland in a similar case involving dry rot: *Robbie v Graham & Sibbald* (1989). The judge (reluctantly) held—partly on an interpretation of Part II UCTA, which only applies in Scotland—that such a disclaimer was not a notice having contractual effect. Where it was clear and unambiguous it was not struck at by UCTA. However, as from April 1, 1991 any provision in a non-contractual notice does come under the provisions of UCTA by virtue of the Law Reform (Miscellaneous Provisions)(Scotland) Act 1990, s.68. The case of *Robbie* was effectively reversed by the statutory provision.

THE "BATTLE OF FORMS"

It is common for businesses when sending an order, *i.e.* an offer, to do so subject to their own standard pre-printed conditions. That in itself causes no major problem. The problem really begins when the second party accepts the offer on its own standard form acceptance—and the terms of offer and acceptance do not meet and may even contradict. Sometimes both sets of conditions may say that, in the event of a dispute, its terms will rule!

To state the obvious, if the parties perform their respective obligations, without problem or dispute, the contents of the small print is really only academic. If, however, a dispute arises, there can be major problems, not least whether or not a contract actually exists. In fact, usually the courts decide there is basic consensus, although that may not always be entirely logical. Frequently, the terms of the contract will be those of the party who "fired the last shot".

The foundation case is *Butler Machine Tool Co. v Ex-Cell-O Corporation* (1979). Sellers of a machine sent their offer to sell on a standard form. It included a clause allowing the seller to increase the price if costs rose prior to delivery. The buyers sent their "acceptance" using their standard form, containing a different set of conditions and incorporating a tear-off portion stating that the sellers accepted the buyer's standard terms. The sellers signed and returned this tear-off portion. Later, the sellers attempted to increase the price, in line with their original offer. The buyers did not consider themselves to be bound by any power to increase the price and queried whether there even was a contract. The court decided that a contract had been formed, but according to the terms of the buyers. Their purported acceptance had really been a counter-offer which the sellers had accepted by returning the tear-off slip. The clause in the original offer, with the rest of that offer, had fallen. The above case has been followed in Scotland in a similar case of *Uniroyal Ltd v Miller & Co. Ltd* (1985).

Sometimes the original offer may contain an overriding clause, stating that the terms of the offer will prevail unless the offeror consents, in writing, to any variation of these terms. There is a sheriff court case confirming the competence of such a clause—*Roofcare Ltd v Gillies* (1984).

---

8. INTERPRETATION, TITLE TO SUE AND ASSIGNATION

INTERPRETATION

> "*'When I use a word,'* Humpty Dumpty said in rather a scornful tone, *'it means just what I choose it to mean—neither more nor less.' 'The question is,'* said Alice, *'whether you can make words mean different things.' 'The question is,'* said Humpty Dumpty, *'which is to be master—that's all.'*"

The above quotation from Lewis Carroll's "Alice in Wonderland" might give the impression that problems of interpretation only take place in books. In Chapter 1, the quotation from a judgement of Lord President Dunedin in *Muirhead & Turnbull v Dickson* (1905), was noted and shows the matter from a different perspective: "commercial contracts cannot be arranged by what people think in their innermost minds. Commercial contracts are arranged according to what people say."

In practice, many written contracts in modern use are clear, unambiguous and free from jargon. Nevertheless, problems are bound to arise from time to time and certain basic rules have emerged, mainly though common law. There have also been statutory inroads, particularly through the Contract (Scotland) Act 1997. However, the starting point in this area is simple. It is assumed that parties say what they mean and mean what they say. In areas of interpretation, words are generally given their ordinary and natural meaning. This traditional approach was taken in *Bank of Scotland v Dunedin Property Investment Co. Ltd* (1999). Nevertheless, that case also suggested that the circumstances in which the words are used may also be taken into account.

If there is more than one possible interpretation, the courts tend to favour the one which gives effect to the contract rather than that which might nullify it. On the other hand, if the wording is too vague, the contract may be unenforceable. Also, as a very general rule, courts do not seek to rewrite contracts for the parties. The normal common law rule is that either a contract term stands or it falls. This is well illustrated by some of the cases considered under *pacta illicita* in Chapter 6. There are times when the court may have statutory power to vary an agreement, as it can in the case of an extortionate credit agreement under the Consumer Credit Act 1974. It is also possible for the court to vary a written document under the Law Reform (Miscellaneous Provisions) (Scotland) Act 1985, s.8, where the document fails to reflect what the parties did actually agree. As demonstrated in Chapter 7, the Unfair Contract Terms Act 1977 limits the effectiveness of exclusion clauses in certain contracts.

The "parole evidence" rule

This, in fact, is a rule which no longer exists, but its long history and its subsequent abolition requires brief comment. At common law, the position was clear. Where a contract had been committed to writing, evidence, whether written or oral, from outside the document purporting to prove that the terms were other than those written, was not admissible. This rule, was derived mainly from a House of Lords case—*Inglis v Buttery* (1878)—but had been subject to many exceptions throughout the years, such as latent ambiguity or usage of trade. The Contract (Scotland) Act 1997 provides a rebuttable presumption that a document contains all the express terms of a contract where it appears so to do. This presumption can be rebutted by contrary extrinsic evidence, *i.e.* from outwith the four corners of the document, that additional terms exist. This evidence may be either written or verbal. However, if the basic contract contains an express provision that it comprises the whole terms of the agreement (an "entire contract" clause), that provision is taken to be conclusive and thus extrinsic evidence cannot be admitted. These provisions also apply to unilateral promises.

There are occasions where statute already implies certain extrinsic terms into a contract. A clear example is the five implied terms in contracts of sale under the Sale of Goods Act 1979.

The *contra proferentem* rule

If a contract contains a term which is unclear or ambiguous, that term will be interpreted *contra proferentem*, *i.e.* against the party seeking to rely on it. This is vigorously applied in relation to exclusion clauses. In *North of Scotland Hydro-Electric Board v Taylor* (1956), a sub-contractor to H-E, was required by his contract to indemnify H-E against "all claims from third parties arising from the operations under contract". Due to the negligence of H-E, one of T's employees was killed by electrocution. The obvious question was whether the clause covered claims arising from H-E's negligence. As the clause was ambiguous on this matter, it was interpreted *contra proferentem* and T was not required to indemnify H-E. In an older case of *Life Association of Scotland v Foster* (1873), ambiguity had been built in to a clause in a life assurance policy. The clause provided that the policy would be void if any statement in the proposal form turned out to be untrue. When the proposer completed the form, she was unaware of already suffering from a potentially terminal condition and stated that she was in good health. After her death, L attempted to avoid payment. As the clause did not make it clear whether the clause was restricted to illness known to the pursuer, it was interpreted *contra proferentum* and L was unable to withhold payment.

Even if a contract term is clear, it seems that it can never protect one party from the consequences of a total breach of contract. This is sometimes referred to as the "doctrine of fundamental breach". In *Pollock v Macrae* (1922), P contracted to build marine engines for M. The contract stated "All goods are supplied on the condition that we shall not be liable for any direct or consequential damages arising from defective material or workmanship, even when such goods are supplied under the usual form of guarantee". This clause would have protected P if parts of the engine had been found to be defective. However, it gave no protection where there was a total breach of contract due to the delivery of unserviceable engines.

The *ejusdem generis* rule

Where there is a list of items, broadly of the same or very similar type, followed by general words such as "and other things" or "etc.", the generality will be confined to items of the same kind (*ejusdem generis*) and characteristics as those already mentioned.

TITLE TO SUE

A basic point about a contract is that it is enforceable between the parties to it. By and large the enforcement or otherwise is a matter only for these parties. This is known as the doctrine of *jus tertii* which, confusingly, translates as "right of a third party". In other words, it is saying that, in general, a third party, even if he has an interest in the contract, has *no* right to enforce it. To put it in more conventional legal language, the third party is said to have no title to sue. In English law, this rule was historically stricter than in Scotland and was known as "privity of contract". The Contract (Rights of Third Parties) Act 1999 made the rights of third parties under English law more or less the same as in Scotland.

The general rule of *jus tertii* is well illustrated in the old case of *Finnie v Glasgow and South-Western Railway* (1857): a contract had been signed between two railway companies, agreeing the rate for the haulage of coal along a particular stretch of railway line. When one of the companies increased its charges, a customer sought, in effect, to enforce the original terms of the contract. The contract between the two railway companies was held to be *jus tertii* so far as that customer was concerned. There was no denying that the customer had an interest in the contract, but he had no title to sue.

Scots law has permitted certain exceptions to the rule of *jus tertii*, now to be examined in turn.

Assignation

If a contract is capable of being assigned (discussed later in this chapter), the assignee stands "in the shoes" of the cedent and has title to sue.

Agency

If an agent, acting within his actual or ostensible authority, makes a contract on behalf of his principal (the person whom he represents), the principal will normally have a title to sue on that contract. Indeed, the general rule is that where an agent forms a contract on behalf of an undisclosed, *i.e.* unnamed, principal and the agent has acted within his authority, that agent is not personally liable to the third party provided he does disclose the identity of his principal when requested to do so. Even if it is arguable that, in all the facts and circumstances, the agent has a degree of personal interest, it is clear that either the principal or the agent (but not both) has a title to sue or be sued. In *Bennett v Inveresk Paper Co.* (1891), B, an Australian newspaper owner and previously undisclosed principal, was entitled to sue for damage to a consignment of paper shipped to Australia on the order of B's London agent who had never disclosed B's existence to the paper supplier. Similarly, if the third party wishes to sue, he must elect between agent or principal. In *Ferrier v Dodds* (1865), F bought a warranted mare from D, an auctioneer, but complained shortly afterwards that the mare was unsound. D invited F to return the mare to her original owner, B, whose identity had not been disclosed at the roup. F did so and later attempted to sue both D and B. It was held that, having returned the mare to B, F had made his election to sue B and could no longer sue D.

Death or Bankruptcy

If either party to a contract dies, any title to sue will pass to his executor, unless the contract involves a particularly personal element, known as *delectus personae* (choice of person) (considered further below)—in which case, the contract dies with him. A similar rule allows a trustee in bankruptcy, whether acting under a trust deed or in a formal sequestration, to continue with contracts previously entered into by the debtor, assuming that the trustee elects to do so and is not precluded by *delectus personae*. The main distinction between the two situations is that if a trustee in bankruptcy elects not to proceed with a contract when he could do so, he may expose the estate to an action for breach of contract. Such an action would not be appropriate where a contract had been terminated by death. Many commercial leases contain a clause to the effect that should the tenant become bankrupt or insolvent, this will automatically "irritate" the lease, *i.e.* nullify it.

Jus quaesitum tertio

This rather grand-sounding phrase, literally translated as "right accruing to a third party" is used to describe those somewhat limited situations where the law does permit a third party to enforce the contract in his own right. Before this can happen, the *tertius* (as such a third party is called) must be able to show that the contract itself refers to him either as an individual or as one of a class of people and that the original parties to the contract intended to benefit him. This is a fairly onerous hurdle to clear, but some parties have been successful. In *Lamont v Burnett* (1901), N agreed to purchase L's hotel and also undertook to pay £100 to Mrs L, for her assistance when he had visited to inspect the premises. L accepted the entire offer, but B failed to pay Mrs L the £100. She was held entitled to sue B separately for that sum. The case of *Morton's Trustees v Aged Christian Friend Society* (1899) was considered in Chapter 2. In another part of the judgement on that case, it was held that the Society could sue under the contract even though the Society had only been in formation when M had agreed with a steering committee to make certain annual payments to fund charitable pensions.

It is probably fair comment to say that each case would have to be looked at as a whole and according to facts and circumstances. If, for example, rights are intimated to a third party and the first and second parties do not object, this might imply a *jus quaesitum tertio*. In *Carmichael v Carmichael's Executrix* (1920), a father paid premiums to an insurance company, *i.e.* the contract was between the father as first party and the insurers as second party. The contract stated that a sum of money would be paid to the son's executors on his death provided he lived to age 21 and took over the premiums. The son died testate, aged 21, but before paying the first premium or taking delivery of the policy. An aunt was his sole beneficiary. Although the son had never been a party to the insurance, he had acquired a *jus quaesitum tertio* and the aunt was entitled to the proceeds. Contrast that case with *Burr v Commissioners of Bo'ness* (1896). An official had his salary raised at a council meeting. At the next meeting, the council revoked the earlier decision. The official had no right, in law, to the increase since it had not been intimated to him.

A misrepresentation, whether innocent or fraudulent, gives no title to sue except to the person to whom it was addressed. In *Edinburgh United Breweries Ltd v Molleson* (1894), M agreed to sell a brewery to D, the price being based on accounts which were fraudulent. Unaware of the fraud, D resold the business to E. Later, E and D raised an action to reduce the original contract between M and D. Since E had not been the victim of the misrepresentation, nor a party to the contract, they had no title to sue.

Contracts which "run with the land"
In Scotland, it is usual to find that heritable property has certain burdens and conditions attached to it. In the case of a dwelling house, there may well be conditions (agreed by original buyer and seller) which state that the house and garden may only be used for private residential purposes. In a tenement property, there is invariably some provision as to share of upkeep and common repairs, particularly to the roof. Most burdens and conditions are unexceptionable. If these burdens and conditions are *real* (able to be enforced or defended against the world in general), as distinct from being merely personal, they will "run with the land" so that even when ownership changes, the obligations remain. The successors in the title succeed to the rights and duties of those who made the original agreement about conditions. It is generally assumed that co-proprietors in

a tenement property have a *jus quaesitum tertio* and can enforce conditions affecting common repairs and maintenance against one another. This is a specialised area, beyond the realistic scope of this book. It is likely to undergo major changes in the light of the abolition of feudal tenure and Scottish Law Commission recommendations on the future of real burdens and the law of the tenement.

Joint and several liability

This concerns liability when being sued rather than title to sue, but may be conveniently considered at this point. A contract may involve one of the parties being, in fact, more than one person. A particularly common example is partnership. Although a firm is a "person" under Scots law (Chapter 3), it is not entirely separated from the partners who make it up. Thus, if suing a firm for a money debt, the correct procedure is first to sue the firm, failing which the partners. However, it is not necessary to divide the debt amongst the partners. The creditor is entitled to pursue any one of the partners for the full amount. If that partner satisfies the debt, he may claim "relief", *i.e.* proportionate repayment, from his fellow partners. Joint and several liability is common, either by implication of law or by agreement. As well as in partnership, it is found in the ownership of shared property (as in a tenement house) and in cautionary obligations.

ASSIGNATION OF CONTRACT

One party to a contract may well wish to substitute a third party in his place while the contract is still running. It may be possible to delegate performance to a third party, with the consent of the original creditor (Chapter 10). Alternatively, it may be necessary to assign rights of performance to a third party as security for an obligation. An obvious example is a contract of insurance being used as a security for a debt. Thus John Smith might have an endowment life policy with Casualty Insurance. He wishes to assign it in security for a loan from Rockhard Finance. Smith is referred to as the *cedent* and Rockhard Finance is the *assignee*. Somewhat confusingly, Casualty Insurance is traditionally referred to as the *debtor*, namely the party due to pay or perform under the contract of insurance.

Which contracts can be assigned?

If all that remains to be performed is payment for, or delivery of, a particular item, that right to receive performance can be assigned without the debtor's consent, unless the parties originally agreed otherwise. This is known as an *executed* contract. However, in the case of an *executorial* contract, performance has still to take place. Whether executorial contracts can be assigned is a matter of fact as well as law and hinges on the crucial concept of *delectus personae* alluded to above and now further considered.

Delectus personae

Choice of person can be inferred where one party enters a contract relying on the personal qualities of the other. Where there is an element of *delectus personae*, performance of the element relying on it cannot be assigned. The stereotyped examples are employment and partnership, painting a portrait or even writing a book like this! Usually, common sense is a good guide as to whether there is *delectus personae*. Occasionally, there may be an element of doubt, particularly in respect of delivery of goods. *Cole v Handasyde & Co* (1910): S sold H a quantity of black grease. S was an expert on the commodity, although he did not manufacture it. Before the grease could be delivered, S was declared bankrupt. H refused to accept delivery of the grease from C, S's trustee in bankruptcy, maintaining that he had only entered the contract in reliance on S's personal skill. C was entitled to take over that contract, as it did not rely on S's skill or experience in such a way as to make him *delectus personae*.

The effect of assignation

When a contract can be validly assigned, the assignee enjoys the same rights as the cedent possessed. There is a legal maxim *assignatus utitor jure auctoris* (the assignee enjoys the right of his cedent). Less formally, it is said that the assignee "stands in the shoes" of the cedent. This means that the assignee acquires no better right than the cedent himself had. If there was some flaw or vitiating factor in the original contract, the assignee takes it subject to that possible right of challenge. *Scottish Widows' Fund v Buist* (1876): M took out a policy on his own life with S but made false statements as to his health and, in particular, his drinking habits. He subsequently assigned the policy in security to B and others. When M died at age 30, S not only declined to pay the sum assured to B but also succeeded in an action to reduce the insurance contract on the grounds of the original false statements. Since the original contract was void as between S and M, it was also void as against B. Similarly, in *Johnstone-Beattie v Dalziel* (1868), a father put certain sums in trust through his daughter's marriage-contract, these to be paid to her husband on the father's death. The husband assigned this money in security to his creditors, but on his subsequent divorce his rights to it were forfeited, as were the rights of his creditors.

Method of assignation

Under the Requirements of Writing (Scotland) Act 1995, it is not essential for assignations to be put in writing. Common sense indicates that, in practice, they will be written. Prior to the 1995 Act, assignations counted as one of the *obligationes literis* (see Chapter 2). The writing may take the statutory form prescribed by the Transmission of Moveable Property (Scotland) Act 1862 although, in practice, less formal styles are frequently used. In *Brownlea v Robb* (1907) the written words "I hand over my life policy to my daughter" provided a valid assignation. The transfer of many of the more common examples of contractual and other rights may be governed by particular statutory provision, such as for insurance policies under the Policies of Insurance Act 1867 or for stocks and shares under the Stock Transfer Act 1963.

It is important to understand that even when a right is assigned, the assignee's right against the cedent is only personal. To make his right real, the assignee must intimate the assignation to the "debtor" (as explained above). Any competing priority of right is governed by the date of intimation, not the dates of the documents of assignation. To go back to the earlier fictitious example, if John Smith wishes to assign his insurance policy in security to Rockhard Finance, he signs and delivers an assignation in their favour. Rockhard will then make their right real by intimating the assignation to the "debtor", *i.e.* Casualty Insurance. This intimation should be made in writing. The normal practice is to send the intimation in duplicate with the request that one copy be returned, stamped as acknowledged. Occasionally, even if there has been no express intimation, the debtor may be personally barred from denying knowledge of the assignation if he has acted, or refrained from acting, in a particular way.

Negotiable instruments
A right under a negotiable instrument passes with the instrument itself and is not affected by the *assignatus* rule referred to above. These negotiable instruments include bills of exchange, cheques, promissory notes and banknotes. The "holder in good faith and for value" of such an instrument, such as someone who has had a cheque endorsed over to him, is not affected by a defect in title to that instrument earlier in the chain of negotiation, provided it was not originally void. Thus, a shopkeeper who, in good faith and in the course of business, accepts a banknote which turns out to have been stolen in an armed robbery, is still entitled to retain it. If, however, the banknote is a forgery it is worthless *ab initio* (from the beginning) and the defect has not arisen in the chain of negotiation. Since the passing of the Cheques Act 1992, cheques which are crossed "A/C payee only" cannot be made negotiable.

CONTRACT (SCOTLAND) ACT 1997

Mention has already been made of the abolition of the so-called "parole evidence" rule by s.1 of the 1997 Act. The Act did not provide any comprehensive reform or codification of the Scottish common law of contract. It sought to abolish "three bad rules" identified in a report by the Scottish Law Commission (No. 152) published in 1996. For the sake of completeness, the two other changes, which principally affect conveyancing practice, are now dealt with briefly.

Section 2 abolished the "rule in *Winston v Patrick*" (1980) that missives for the sale of heritable property were superseded ("killed off") by the delivery of the conveyance of the property. This was not an academic point, since modern missives are often complex documents bristling with conditions about the state of central heating, drainage and electrical wiring, to say nothing of demanding delivery of a bewildering selection of documents. In order to ensure that these missive conditions were kept "alive", notwithstanding the delivery of the disposition, it became customary for the missives to contain a clause continuing their effective life for a period of time, usually two years, after delivery of the disposition. As a result of a plethora of conflicting sheriff court cases, it subsequently became almost universal practice to insert a non-supersession clause in the disposition itself. Since the 1997 Act came into force, this is no longer required.

The execution of a deed in implement of a previous contract does not, of itself, supersede unimplemented or unfulfilled terms of that contract—unless parties agree otherwise. The practice has emerged among sellers' agents of inserting a "supersession clause" in the missives, in order to ensure that after a period of time, usually two years, the buyer can no longer found on missive provisions. This is to avoid sellers having obligations possibly extending over an unacceptably long period of time.

Until the passing of the Act, it seemed that a buyer of heritable property or a business did not have a right in law to keep the property and claim damages if it turned out to be defective—*Fortune v Fraser* (1996). Either he had to keep the property and claim no damages or reject it and claim damages. Unlike a buyer of goods, who has the protection of the Sale of Goods Act 1979, ss.15B and 53A, he did not have recourse to the *actio quanti minoris* which, very loosely translated, means "something off the price". Section 3 of the 1997 Act provides that a buyer who retains defective property may obtain damages for the seller's breach of contract. It used to be common practice for missives of sale to provide expressly for the *actio quanti minoris* to be implied into the contract. Such a provision is now unnecessary.

---

9. REMEDIES FOR BREACH OF CONTRACT

At this stage, it is assumed that a contract has been validly formed and is free from vitiating factors. Fortunately, the majority of contracts are performed uneventfully but, unless human nature changes radically, there will always be some defaulters. When one of the parties to a contract fails to carry out his side of the obligation, he will be considered in breach of contract, unless the reasons for his non-performance are recognised as valid in law, *e.g.* supervening impossibility, considered in Chapter 10.

Breach can arise, in practice, in three different ways: (1) total non-performance, (2) partial performance or (3) defective performance. When a breach arises, what remedies in law does the party not in breach (the "innocent" party) have? He will have a right to claim damages but he may also have other rights over and above. The main remedies and defensive measures are specific implement and interdict, rescission, retention, lien or action for payment. These will now be examined in turn.

SPECIFIC IMPLEMENT AND INTERDICT

It is an innocent party's basic right in law to ask the court for a decree to make the party in breach fulfil the terms of his obligation under the contract. If the action is in the positive, *i.e.* to make the party in breach do something, the court may award a decree *ad factum praestandum* (for the performance of an act) which means, quite literally, that the party must specifically implement his contractual obligations. If the action is in the negative, *i.e.* to stop the party in breach from doing something he agreed not to do, the court may award a decree of interdict. If an employer wanted to prevent a former employee from working for a competitor, in breach of a restrictive covenant, he could use such a remedy as in *Bluebell Apparel v Dickinson* (1980) considered in Chapter 6. Interdict can never be used to enforce a positive obligation. In *Church Commissioners for England v Abbey National plc* (1994), AN intended closing a branch office. C, the landlords, considered this to be in breach of the lease. However, they were unable to make AN keep the branch open by means of the remedy of interdict. It is, however, possible to specifically implement a positive obligation in a lease to "keep open" certain premises, provided it is not impossible nor unreasonable—*Retail Parks Investments Ltd v The Royal Bank of Scotland plc (No 2)* (1996) followed in *Highland and Universal Properties Ltd v Safeway Properties Ltd* (2000).

If the party in breach wilfully fails to obey the decree, whether it be positive or negative, he puts himself in contempt of court, the result of which could be a fine or even imprisonment. In practice, the court rarely takes these draconian steps. If there is apparent non-compliance, the court will expect an explanation but will listen to reason and normally give sufficient time to allow the party in default to put matters right.

Under Scots law, specific implement is, in theory, the primary remedy to which an innocent party is entitled in the case of breach of contract. In practice, it is not a particularly common remedy. In addition, there are quite a number of situations where the courts do not consider specific implement as an equitable or suitable remedy and will not grant a decree as a matter of course. The following are the main areas where a court will *not* grant a decree *ad factum praestandum*.

1. Where the obligation is to *pay a sum of money*. A debtor in default could find himself in contempt of court and thus liable to imprisonment for non-payment. As a matter of public policy, debtors are not normally sent to prison. In Scotland, a creditor can enforce payment by simpler processes, such as action for payment and diligence.

2. Where a contract involves *personal relationships* which it would be better not to enforce, *e.g.* employment or partnership. If A and B are business partners and B does not wish the partnership to continue, common

sense indicates that there is nothing to be gained by A taking B to court and trying to force the issue. In *Skerret v Oliver* (1896) a minister of a presbyterian church had been suspended from office. He asked the court for a decree *ad factum praestandum* to force the church to reinstate him, but this was not an appropriate remedy. Similarly, in the English case of *Page One Records Ltd v Britton (t/a The Troggs)* (1967), the manager of a pop group was unable to keep his post by court action as the members of the group had lost confidence in him. Under employment legislation, an employee who has been unfairly dismissed may, occasionally, be awarded reinstatement by an industrial tribunal. The common law position, however, is as above.

3. Where the subject matter of the contract has *no special significance in itself*, such as 100 bags of flour. The remedy for the innocent party would be to rescind (*i.e.* call off) the contract, obtain the same goods elsewhere and claim damages. An action *ad factum praestandum* could be appropriate if the contract concerned a specific item such as a unique painting, as that is said to have a *pretium affectionis* (price of affection) *i.e.* a value in itself.

4. Where the contract is *illegal or impossible* to perform or where the court could not enforce the decree, *e.g.* if the party in breach is furth of Scotland.

5. Where, in the opinion of the court, it would be *unjust* to grant such a remedy.

At common law, an interdict can be obtained quite speedily on an interim basis. Although there is no such common law equivalent in the case of specific implement, there are appropriate statutory provisions under the Court of Session Act 1988. In either case, the award is at the discretion of the court and without prejudice to its decision at a subsequent hearing.

RESCISSION

The innocent party may, in certain circumstances, bring the contract to an end without going near a court of law. Clearly, if such a remedy was too widely available, it would favour "hotheads" who would be happy enough to call off a contract for the slightest and most trivial of reasons.

For rescission to be appropriate, the breach must be material and go to the root of the contract. An inappropriate rescission counts as a repudiation and can give rise to a claim in damages. *Wade v Waldon* (1909): Wade, a famous comedian, better known by his stage name "George Robey", contracted with Waldon to appear in one year's time at a Glasgow theatre. A clause in the contract provided that Wade was to give 14 days notice before the performance and also to supply publicity material. He failed to do either. Waldon called off the entire contract, although Wade was more than willing to appear at the theatre as agreed. Wade was in breach of contract, but it was not a material breach and could not justify rescission on Waldon's part. The essence of the contract was Wade's appearing on stage, which he had always been willing to do. Waldon was thus liable in damages, as he had repudiated the contract.

Rescission means the justifiable cancellation of a contract. By contrast, repudiation is the unilateral act of a party to a contract whereby he indicates, expressly or by implication, that he does not intend to perform his part of the obligation. It would then be open to the innocent party to rescind the contract in view of the material breach, and claim damages. Total non-performance would always be material, provided it was definite. If the innocent party still wishes the party in breach to perform, obviously he will not rescind as long as he believes that there is life in the contract. The verb of rescission is "rescind". Sometimes, particularly in the area of contracts to buy and sell heritable property, the verb used is "resile"; the two verbs appear to mean the same thing.

In any contract, both parties are bound to perform their respective obligations. The implication is that one party cannot insist on performance by the other if he himself is not willing to carry out his part of the agreement. An employee is entitled to pay for duties performed but if he chooses to take an afternoon off, without permission, he cannot expect to be paid for it. *Graham v United Turkey Red Co.* (1922): a contract of agency dated in 1914 provided that G was to sell only cotton goods made by UTR, in return for payment on a commission basis. From 1916 onwards, G sold goods made by other manufacturers and was thus in breach of contract. G was only entitled to commission up to 1916, *i.e.* up to the time when he himself was still keeping faith with his obligation, but not for the period thereafter. Material breach was also held to occur when a club manager refused to carry out certain tasks in the honest, but mistaken, belief that they were not part of his duties—*Blyth v Scottish Liberal Club* (1983).

There is a further complication. If the innocent party rescinds, he cannot then enforce performance of any part of the contract. He can only claim damages. In the case of *Lloyds Bank plc v Bamberger* (1994), the innocent party rescinded a contract and then sought certain interest payments, as specified in the contract, from the defaulting party. This was not possible since the innocent party had rescinded the entire contract and could not now seek to invoke parts of it. This decision is in line with the established legal principle of approbate and reprobate, which means that a party cannot take advantage of one part of a written document and reject the remainder. However, provisions can be built in to a contract which keep certain parts of it alive, even if the material parts are rescinded. This requires careful draughtsmanship and most qualified acceptances of offers to buy heritable property routinely contain a "Lloyds Bank" clause.

Clearly, one of the problems in this whole area is knowing when a breach of contract is material. Parties may agree between themselves at the outset which breaches would count as material. In some cases it will be clearly implied. Common sense dictates that a wedding dress would normally be required by a bride in time for her wedding. In such a case, it is said that *time is of the essence* of the contract. Usually, however, time is not of the essence unless expressly stated to be so or circumstances, such as the involvement of perishable goods, make it clear that it is implied. In contracts for the sale of heritable property, payment of the purchase price on the date of entry is not of the essence, at common law. *Rodger (Builders) Ltd v Fawdry* (1950): F agreed to sell land to R, with entry at November 11, 1947. R failed to pay at the date of entry. A fortnight later, F warned R that the agreement to sell would be at an end unless payment was made in full by November 28. Payment was not made on the 28th and F immediately agreed to sell the same subjects to B. F was not entitled to rescind merely because of a delay in payment.

This does not mean that parties are expected to wait for ever for contracts to be performed. The normal practice is to issue a "warning" to the other side and, frequently, impose a reasonable time limit for performance. As shown in the previous case, that time limit must be reasonable. In the sale of heritable property, it is common for the seller to qualify his acceptance by stating that time is of the essence as regards payment in full at the date of entry.

Particular problems can arise where the breach is one of several stipulations as in *Wade v Waldon* (1909)(above) or involves defective performance. Just how defective does performance have to be to count as material breach? At common law, that is not always easy to answer. Sometimes a statute itself may give guidance, such as the Sale of Goods Act 1979, s.15B.

In contracts of lease, it is common to find an *irritancy* or termination clause which allows the landlord to irritate, *i.e.* end, the lease in the event of specified breaches by the tenant. There have been cases in the past where the remedy has been abused and the landlord's right to irritate cannot now be exercised unless the tenant is given at least 14 days written notice in the case of a monetary breach. In the case of non-monetary breach, the court will only confirm the irritancy if the landlord has acted in a reasonable manner. (Law Reform (Miscellaneous Provisions)(Scotland) Act 1985, ss.4–7)

RETENTION

Retention is the withholding of payment of a money debt until such time as the other party performs his obligation in full, *e.g.* a tenant may wish to withhold his payment of rent until the landlord carries out his legal duty to put the house in a habitable condition. There are some restrictions as to when this measure can be used since, as a general rule of law, a debtor cannot refuse to pay a debt simply because he has another claim against the creditor. Retention, like lien (below), is not so much a remedy as a defensive measure. Retention can only be used in the following situations:

1. Where both claims arise under the same contract (as in the example of landlord and tenant given above).

2. Where "compensation" can be pleaded, *i.e.* both debts must be liquid (actually due and of an ascertained amount) and the parties are debtor and creditor in the same capacity at the same time. To put this another way, there has to be *concursus debiti et crediti* (concurrence of debt and credit). *Stuart v Stuart* (1869): Col. S brought an action against his brother, Revd S, for repayment of an alleged loan. Revd S alleged that Col. S had received large

advances from their late father and that, as executor of their father, he (Revd S) had counterclaims against Col. S for more than the alleged loan. Revd S could not plead the alleged counterclaims in compensation, there being no *concursus debiti et crediti*. The office of executor denotes a different capacity from the same person acting as a private individual.

3. Where the creditor in a money obligation is bankrupt.

LIEN

Lien (pronounced "lean") is the withholding of property which would normally be delivered to the other party. There are two kinds of lien, general and special. The special lien is by far the more common. In outline, a special lien allows a person who has done work on the moveable property of another, or has not been paid the purchase price of goods, to retain possession of that property until he has received the payment due. So, if X takes his car to be repaired and is unable to pay the bill when he calls to collect it, the garage may well retain his car until payment is made. This is exercising a right of lien against these "special" or specific goods. Two other points should be noted:

1. Lien is a possessory right. The car in the above example, does not become the property of the garage, it is merely in the garage's possession. Furthermore, if the garage proprietor does let X take his car away without paying the bill, he cannot later re-exercise the lien. In *Hostess Mobile Catering v Archibald Scott Ltd* (1981), S sold H a piece of catering equipment, but the item was not paid for in full. When it was returned to S for repairs under guarantee, S unsuccessfully attempted to re-exercise their right of lien.

2. A special lien can only be exercised against the goods which are specific or special to the contract. Much less common is the general lien which allows the holder of the article to retain it until a general balance due by the owner of the goods is satisfied. Certain trades and professions have the right in law to do this but the courts do not favour any extension of these categories. A law agent would, say, be entitled to retain title deeds and share certificates in his possession until a client had paid his professional account for drawing up a new will. *Paul v Meikle* (1868): Mrs D bequeathed certain heritable property to her son. The will had been drawn up by M, Mrs D's solicitor, who was also her creditor in respect of unpaid professional fees extending over many years. M was entitled to retain the will until his fees were paid. A solicitor's right of lien is well established, being traced back to the old case of *Ranking of Hamilton of Provenhall's Creditors* (1781). However, in *Christie v Ruxton* (1862), it was held that the lien did not cover cash advances made by a solicitor to his client. When a document or title deed subject to lien is the property of sequestrated debtor, the permanent trustee in the sequestration can, under s.38(4) of the Bankruptcy (Scotland) Act 1985, require delivery of the document in question. This is without prejudice to any right of preference to which the lien holder is entitled. In practice, it is relatively simple to defeat a lien over a document if it is of a

type where a duplicate or certified copy can be obtained. It seems that an accountant does not enjoy a right of general lien, although it is well established that he has right of special lien—*Meikle & Wilson v Pollard* (1880). A banker has a general lien on bills of exchange, cheques and promissory notes belonging to a customer provided these have come into his possession in the course of banking transactions. This general lien does not extend to articles left with the bank for safe keeping. An innkeeper has a general lien over a guest's luggage, pending payment of the hotel bill.

Although it is only a defensive measure, lien is common in practice and highly persuasive in making payment forthcoming. It is particularly useful where the innocent party does not wish to rescind or where it would be pointless to do so because he has, in fact, performed his part of the contract.

ACTION FOR PAYMENT

Although some legal textbooks might convey a different impression, the most common breach of contract is non-payment of money. As explained above, specific implement would not be an appropriate remedy for pursuing a money debt. A short delay in payment is not necessarily material breach. It is sometimes a fine line between delay in payment and actual non-payment. Thus rescission must not be exercised too hastily. In any event, it would normally be inept to rescind a contract unless *restitutio in integrum* (restoration of parties to their original position) were possible. Where the contract price is unpaid but goods have been delivered or services performed, the creditor can recover payment by means of a court action. Most such actions are undefended. The creditor would then be able to enforce his decree by diligence.

The Late Payment of Commercial Debts (Interest) Act 1998 has given rights to businesses to charge interest on late payment of money debts due by other businesses or by bodies in the public sector. Whilst parties can contract out of these provisions, they can only do so *after* the creation of the debt.

DAMAGES

"It is impossible to say that a contract can be broken, even in respect of time, without the party being entitled to claim damages—at the lowest, nominal damages." These are the often quoted words of Lord President Inglis in *Webster & Co. v Cramond Iron Co.* (1875). Under Scots law, wherever there is an established breach of contract, however small and no matter what other remedies or measures have been used by the pursuer, a claim for damages is always open. In the real world, the innocent party, in the case of a minor breach, is unlikely to pursue the other party through the law courts with a claim for damages, but that possibility is always there.

The purpose of damages is simple: it is to compensate the innocent party for his loss and to place him in the position he would have been in had the contract been fully performed, in so far as money alone is capable of doing this. This means that the actual breach of contract must have caused some loss. In *Irving v Burns* (1915), B, secretary of a picture-house company, engaged Irving to carry out certain plumber work, although B had no authority to do so. Irving performed his part of the contract but received no payment since, by now, the company was hopelessly insolvent. He then sued B for damages since, at common law, an agent is said to "warrant his authority" and it was now clear that B had been given no authority to form the contract. Irving was unsuccessful. He had undoubtedly suffered a loss but it was not due to B's breach of warranty of authority. If the contract had been properly formed, Irving would have received no payment, since the company was insolvent. He was thus no worse off as a result of B's conduct.

Even if no actual loss has been sustained, the court may award nominal damages to compensate for trouble and inconvenience. In practice, no one normally raises an action for nominal damages, unless very determined to make a point of principle, since such damages are only awarded in respect of non-pecuniary loss. In *Webster* (above), C agreed to supply pipes for a cotton mill. There was a delay of three months in supplying them. W, the mill owners, claimed £300 damages for the loss sustained by the delay but they were unable to prove that they had, in fact, suffered any financial loss. They were able to prove, however, that they had been put to considerable trouble and inconvenience. They were awarded nominal damages of £10.

In more recent times, the courts have shown an increasing willingness to award more realistic damages in respect of the irritation and disappointment which can be caused by breach of contract. Realistic amounts were awarded in *Jarvis v Swan Tours* (1973), where there was a disastrous failure by a tour company to match the expectations arising from its brochure. There was a similar result in *Deisen v Samson* (1971), where a photographer failed to turn up at a wedding to which many guests had travelled from Norway and had worn their national costume.

There are three important points to note about damages:

1. Damages are never to be considered as a penalty or civil punishment of the party in breach. There is no place for so-called "punitive" damages in Scots law. The purpose of damages, as stated above, is to compensate the innocent party for loss incurred.

2. The innocent party is expected to take reasonable steps to minimise his loss, *i.e.* to keep it as low as possible, otherwise his claim for damages could be restricted to the amount he could have claimed if he had taken such steps. Thus, if a party is not supplied with goods, but then delays in buying in suitable goods elsewhere until the price has risen, his claim for damages will be restricted. *Ireland v Merryton Coal Co.* (1894): a wholesaler agreed to supply retail coal merchants with a large quantity of coal to be delivered "over the next four months" in "average" or "about equal" monthly quantities. By the end of the four-month period, the wholesaler had only supplied about half of the total consignment. The retailers claimed damages on the basis of the market price ruling at the end of the four months. The price had risen over the period. In other words, the retailers had not taken all

reasonable steps to minimise their loss, so their claim for damages was restricted.

However, the innocent party is only expected to take reasonable steps to minimise his loss. He does not have to take extraordinary steps. Thus in *Gunther v Lauritzen* (1894), L had agreed to sell a cargo of Dutch hay to G. The latter intended to resell the hay in consignments to his customers. L failed to supply goods of the required quality but when he was sued for damages, claimed that G could have obtained the goods elsewhere and that he had not minimised his loss. In fact, the commodity was in very scarce supply and could only have been obtained by buying in small amounts from various suppliers throughout the country. The court found that minimisation of loss did not require such an onerous demand. The innocent party was only required to take reasonable steps.

3. The *quantum* (how much) of damages is worked out on the principle that only loss which is a direct and foreseeable result of the breach of contract can be claimed. Damages in that case are referred to as "general" or "ordinary" damages. If there are special or "knock-on" circumstances which lead to an unusual or special loss, the party in breach is not held liable, *i.e.* to pay special damages, unless he knew of the special circumstances at the time the contract was formed. The basic effect is that a party in breach of contract will not normally be liable for all the consequences of his breach. This basic principle is often referred to as the "rule in *Hadley v Baxendale*" (1854). H's flour mill was at a standstill because the cast-iron crankshaft from a steam engine had fractured. The broken crankshaft had to be sent from the mill in Gloucester to a foundry at Greenwich, to be used as a pattern for a replacement. B, a carrier, was given the task of transporting it. He was told that it was a crankshaft for a mill but he was not made aware that, on account of the broken crankshaft, the mill was at a standstill. Most mills normally kept a spare. B was negligent and caused a delay in delivering the new crankshaft. He was in breach of contract, because he had undertaken to complete his work within two days. However, H was not entitled to claim special damages for the loss of profits when the mill was at a standstill because these special circumstances had not been properly explained to B when the contract was formed. Thus, this special loss of profit was beyond what the carrier could have been expected to foresee. Some further case law may illustrate how the courts have interpreted this rule in practice.

Victoria Laundry v Newman Industries (1949): N agreed to supply a boiler to V, who required it (a) to expand their business and (b) to permit them to take up a large government contract. The boiler was delivered late, by which time the government contract had been lost. As N had no way of knowing about the government contract when they agreed to supply the boiler, they were only liable for ordinary or general damages for the foreseeable loss of business and not for any special damages in respect of the lost contract.

Den of Ogil Co. Ltd v Caledonian Railway Co. (1902): the "Den of Ogil", a steamship of 4000 tons lying at Plymouth, had broken one of her pistons. A replacement had been cast at Port Glasgow and was sent by passenger train to Plymouth. The railway company were informed that the carriage was urgent and that delay would cause detention of the ship. However, they were not informed that it was such a large ship which had 57 crewmen on board, nor were they told that the casting was a piston. There was a delay of some three or four days in delivery. The ship owner sued the railway company for damages, including outlays and loss of profits. The railway company were liable for general damages in respect of the part of the outlays caused by the delay, but not for special damages in respect of the loss of profit.

Macdonald v Highland Railway Co. (1873): confectionery for the celebration of the coming of age of Lord Macdonald on the Isle of Skye was sent by rail from Inverness via Dingwall and Strome Ferry. The cartons containing the confectionery were clearly marked "PERISHABLE", thus clearly bringing the railway company's attention to the special circumstances of the contract. Due to the company's negligence, the cartons were held up at Dingwall. When eventually they reached Skye, the celebration was past and the confectionery had perished. The railway company were liable for all the loss, because the special circumstances, *i.e.* that the goods were perishable, had been clearly brought to their notice at the time the contract was formed.

Hobbs v London & South Western Railway Co. (1875): H, with his wife and two children, caught the last train from Wimbledon to Hampton Court. The train took the wrong line and they had to get off at a different station. It was too late to obtain alternative transport or to put up at an inn. The family had to walk five miles home in the rain, arriving back around 3.00 a.m. As a result, Mrs H caught a severe cold and was unable to assist her husband in his business for some time. Damages amounting to £8 were awarded for the inconvenience of walking home in the rain. However, no special damages could be awarded in respect of Mrs H's illness and its consequences since these were not the probable and foreseeable results of a breach of contract at the time when it was formed, *i.e.* when Mr H bought the tickets.

Balfour Beatty Construction (Scotland) Ltd v Scottish Power plc (1994): B were constructing a concrete aqueduct to carry the Union Canal over a by-pass. This required a long "continuous pour" of concrete. Work on the first stage was almost complete when the electricity supply failed. As a result, the first stage had to be entirely demolished. B claimed special damages of over a quarter of a million pounds against S. In the House of Lords, B lost their case. It would have required a high degree of technical knowledge of the construction industry on the part of S for them to have foreseen the results of an interruption of the electricity supply.

LIQUIDATE DAMAGES

In the cases considered so far, the courts have been required to assess the *quantum* of damages to be paid when a breach of contract has taken place. Parties can, however, agree at the outset how much will be paid as damages in the event of a breach taking place. This is particularly common in contracts involving building or contracting work, *e.g.* to cover loss incurred through delays in completion. This form of damages is called liquidate damages and is perfectly legitimate and enforceable provided it is a genuine pre-estimate of loss. Confusingly, such a provision in a contract is often called a "penalty clause". This is an unsatisfactory title since, as demonstrated above, damages for breach of contract are intended to be compensatory, not penal.

In fact, the name given to the clause is unimportant. What matters is its actual effect. If it is clear that the clause is intended to punish rather than to compensate, then it is invalid and unenforceable. In such a case, the court would have to assess damages using the usual criteria. On the other hand, where there is a genuine liquidate damages clause, whatever it may actually be called, the amount recoverable by the innocent party is restricted to that amount even if the actual loss is larger or smaller than the sum specified.

In distinguishing between penalty clauses and liquidate damages clauses, the courts have frequently had regard to the principles set out in *Dunlop Pneumatic Tyre Co. v New Garage and Motor Co.* (1915), per Lord Dunedin, which can be summarised as follows:

(a) The use of the words "penalty" or "liquidate damages" is not conclusive in itself.
(b) A penalty punishes; liquidate damages is a genuine pre-estimate of loss.
(c) Whether a sum is a penalty or liquidate damages is a question judged at the time of the formation of the contract, not at the time of the alleged breach.
(d) If a sum is clearly extravagant, it will be counted as penal and thus unenforceable.
(e) If the same single lump sum is payable on the occurrence of several different situations, it will be presumed to be penal.

Lord Elphinstone v Monkland Iron & Coal Co (1886): tenants in a mineral lease had undertaken to level and soil-over deposits of slag by a certain date under a "penalty of £100 per imperial acre for all ground not so restored". The sum was liquidate damages, not a penalty and was enforceable. In other words it was a genuine pre-estimate of loss. *Cameron-Head v Cameron & Co* (1919): in a contract between a firm of timber merchants and the proprietor of an estate, the former bought standing timber on the understanding that the wood was to be cleared by April 1918 under a "penalty of 10s. per day until such is done". By April 1919, the wood had still not been cleared. An action was raised for a year's "penalty". The "penalty" of 10s. (50p) per day was a reasonable pre-estimate and enforceable. *Dingwall v Burnett* (1912): a lease of a hotel in Dunbar provided for a "penalty of £50" to be paid in the event of a breach of any of the lease provisions. The tenant totally non-performed his part of the contract but maintained that he was only liable to pay the £50 "penalty". The court found that the £50 was a penalty and thus unenforceable. This left the way open for the landlord to claim a higher amount according to the normal rules for assessing the *quantum* of damages.

Finally, and very rarely, there could be circumstances in which it is impossible to give a genuine pre-estimate of loss. If this is so, any sum agreed on by the parties will be accepted as liquidate damages, even if in normal circumstances it would appear penal. *Clydebank Engineering and Shipbuilding Co. v Castaneda* (1914): Clydebank, by two contracts, undertook to supply four torpedo-boat destroyers to the Spanish Government. The contract included a clause "The penalty for late delivery shall be at the rate of £500 per week for each vessel not delivered[...]in the contract time". All vessels were delivered many months late. The Spanish Government brought an action against Clydebank for £75,000, calculated in accordance with the "penalty" clause. Clydebank claimed that this provision was penal and thus unenforceable. The remainder of the Spanish fleet had by now been sunk by the Americans off the coast of Cuba. It was accepted that the sum of £500 per week was liquidate damages as it had been impossible to give an accurate pre-estimate of loss at the time the contracts were formed.

It has long been recognised that the law on penalty clauses is in need of modernising. The Scottish Law Commission in its *Report on Penalty Clauses* (No. 171, 1999) has recommended that agreed damages clauses should be enforceable unless manifestly excessive.

ANTICIPATORY BREACH

It might seem strange for a party to a contract to claim a remedy for breach until a breach had actually occurred. However, it is possible that one of the parties could indicate in advance of performance, by his words or actions, that he does not intend to fulfil his obligations. This is known as anticipatory breach.

Suppose a pop singer makes a contract in January to appear at a gig on July 16. On April 1 he states that he will not be coming. He is saying, in other words, that come July 16, he will be in breach of contract. In this situation, what remedies would be open to the promoter? He would actually have a choice: (1) He could treat this as a repudiation of the contract by the singer and could thus rescind, on the grounds of material breach, and claim damages, (2) He could wait until the time of performance and see what happened. In this case, of course, there is no rescission and the contract is kept alive. If the singer does actually appear at the gig, obviously there is no breach of contract. It goes without saying that if the contract is rescinded in April, the damages payable will be much less than if the contract is kept alive and the breach subsequently takes place on July 16.

For an anticipatory breach to take place, the refusal to give performance must be definite. If one party merely expresses doubts about his ability to perform, that is not anticipatory breach. If, in such circumstances, the other party then attempts to rescind, that party could well find himself being sued for damages.

In *White & Carter (Councils) Ltd v McGregor* (1962), W supplied street litter bins to local authorities on condition that W could sell advertising space on the bins. One of W's representatives called at M's garage to arrange a new advertising contract which was to last for three years. Terms were agreed with the garage manager and the contract was duly formed. Later in the day, M telephoned W to cancel the contract. W chose to ignore this purported cancellation. They duly prepared the advertisements and displayed them for the three year period. W were held to have been entitled to proceed with the contract and to sue for the contract price, even although M had already intimated that he would not perform his side of the obligation.

It has to be said that the above case is not without its critics and, although a House of Lords appeal on a Scottish case, the verdict was by a 3:2 majority. It has been pointed out (Woolman and Lake, *Contract* (3rd ed.), p.147) that there is a paradox in the decision since the pursuers were able to overcome the normal principle of minimisation of loss as they were suing for a money debt and not for damages.

The English courts have shown a marked reluctance to follow this decision. In *Clea Shipping Co. v Bulk Oil International (The Alaskan Trader)* (1984), it was held that the innocent party's keeping a ship at anchor off the Piraeus for seven months after an anticipatory breach, was wholly unreasonable. In the Scottish case of *Salaried Staff London Loan Co. Ltd v Swears & Wells* (1985), the *White & Carter* interpretation was followed. In this case, tenants had taken a 34-year lease of premises on an industrial estate but, after the lease had only run for five years, the tenants gave notice that they wished to renounce it. The landlord was entitled to ignore this anticipatory breach. It was stated that only in exceptional circumstances would the court decline to enforce the legal rights of the innocent party. What is meant by "exceptional" would be for the courts themselves to decide in any particular case.

A party choosing to "sit it out" may still be taking a certain risk. In *Avery v Bowden* (1885), the owner of a ship who waited for the expiry of a 45-day period during which the defendant was supposed to be loading a ship, although the latter had already admitted he could not do so, received an unpleasant surprise when the Crimean War broke out. The cargo port was Odessa and the contract was void on the grounds of supervening illegality.

---

10. TERMINATION OF CONTRACT

Early in Chapter 1, it was noted that there is an essential and obvious requirement to have at least two parties to a contract. These parties have reciprocal rights and duties, *i.e.* they are both debtor and creditor to one another. A "debt" is not only an obligation to pay money; it can equally be a duty to perform.

If X agrees to sell goods to Y, we get the following picture. X is Y's debtor, in so far as X is due to deliver goods to Y. X is also Y's creditor, in so far as X is entitled to be paid by Y. Equally, Y is X's debtor, as he is due to pay for the goods, but Y is also X's creditor because he is entitled to have the goods delivered.

When these reciprocal arrangements are satisfied in full, the contract is terminated because it has been carried out in full, *i.e.* performed. Fortunately, the vast majority of contracts are terminated, uneventfully, by performance. However, there are other ways of a contract coming to an end. Strictly speaking, a void contract cannot be ended, because it never existed. Nevertheless, a court may have to declare that the contract is void and make judgement as to the respective rights of parties, as demonstrated in earlier chapters. A voidable contract, as has also been demonstrated, continues to run unless or until it is set aside. If third parties acquire rights under a voidable contract in good faith and for value, that contract cannot be set aside.

It may be that one party is in material breach, allowing the innocent party to rescind and claim damages. The other party may have decided not to perform, *i.e.* to repudiate the contract. Unless it is one of the instances where specific implement is appropriate, the contract will be brought to an end by the innocent party rescinding. If specific implement is appropriate, the contract is, at least in theory, still capable of being performed. The same applies where the defensive measures of retention or lien are used and, in practice, these measures are highly persuasive, as has already been noted.

However, there are other ways in which a contract can be ended and these have a particular significance, in so far as none of them would give rise to any claim for damages. It is these ways which are now to be considered.

PERFORMANCE

As stated above, this is the obvious and the most common way of ending a contract. Partial performance does not count as performance but there is a legal maxim *de minimis not curat lex* (the law does not concern itself with trifles) which means that very minor discrepancies are not suitable matters for litigation nor valid grounds for rescission. Quite frequently, of course, the missing element of performance is payment. Work is done, or goods are delivered, but payment is not forthcoming. Payment should be made in the proper manner, usually at the creditor's place of business or his residence, unless agreed to the contrary. A creditor can insist (again, unless agreed to the contrary) on being paid in what is called legal tender, which under the Coinage Act 1971 (as amended) is:

- £1 or £2 coins up to any amount
- 20p and/or 50p coins up to a maximum of £10
- 10p and/or 5p coins up to a maximum of £5
- bronze up to a maximum of 20p

In Scotland, no Bank of England notes are legal tender. Scottish clearing banks have the historic right to issue their own banknotes but they are not legal tender, even in Scotland. Certain "special issue" coins, such as £5 Crowns, are given the status of legal tender, although few of them pass into normal business coinage.

Payment by credit, charge or "switch" debit card is not legal tender, though very widely accepted, subject to conditions or limits. Payment by cheque is only a conditional payment of a debt. If the cheque is accepted, the money debt is extinguished, but it is revived if the cheque is dishonoured. This is known as a resolutive condition. In *Charge Card Services* (1988), it was held that payment by a credit or charge card counts as absolute and not conditional payment. Consumers had been able to buy petrol from garages by means of a card. The finance company providing the card service went into insolvency. The garages were unable to recover their loss from individual card-holders. The card-holders, however, still had to pay any sums they were due to the liquidator of the insolvent company.

ACCEPTILATION

A debtor may have non-performed or part performed, or even defectively performed his part of the obligation, yet the creditor is prepared to accept this as though it was full performance. The giving of discount is, in fact, a common form of acceptilation.

NOVATION

A creditor and debtor may agree that the debtor will substitute a new obligation for the one originally undertaken, *e.g.* that apples will be supplied instead of pears. It is important that the original obligation is expressly discharged, as there is a general presumption in law against novation. Thus, there is always the danger that the debtor will find himself with two obligations to perform. A debtor has no right to substitute a new obligation unilaterally.

DELEGATION

Delegation is really a form of novation. It involves the substitution of a new debtor, as distinct from a new obligation, in place of the original. It requires the express consent of the creditor and, in any event, would clearly be inappropriate in a contract which has an element of *delectus personae* (choice of person). If someone has arranged for his portrait to be painted by a famous artist, he is unlikely to happy about that "debt" being contracted out to a third party. There is a very general rule that an agent, because his appointment is a matter of personal confidence, has no implied authority to delegate the performance of his duties. This is summed up in the maxim *delegatus non potest delegare* (the one to whom delegation has been made cannot delegate). There are some notable exceptions to the general rule. It is well recognised that a solicitor may delegate the searching of public registers to a professional searcher. Similarly, an architect may delegate measurement of final plans to a surveyor (*Black v Cornelius* (1879)).

CONFUSION

Confusion, occasionally known as "combination", operates where the same person in the same capacity becomes both creditor and debtor in an obligation. It is a basic principle of common law, to say nothing of common sense, that a person cannot be his own debtor. If he finds himself in such a position, the debt is normally extinguished *confusione* (by confusion). Examples are not all that common. Suppose a tenant buys his landlord's right in the property which he occupies as tenant. Clearly, the contract of lease comes to an end as he will not pay himself rent. If, however, the tenant had bought the landlord's right as director of a property company, confusion would not operate. As a tenant, he would be a private individual but as a director he would be acting as a trustee for the company. He would not be debtor and creditor in the same capacity and confusion would not operate.

COMPENSATION

This can be traced back to the Compensation Act 1592. In England, it is usually referred to as "set off". If one party is both debtor and creditor to the other party, he can offset (set off) one claim against the other, reducing or extinguishing the amount due.

If John owes Jean £500 and Jean owes John £200, clearly John will only pay Jean the net sum of £300. However, compensation can only operate if certain conditions are fulfilled:

(1) Compensation must be pleaded in an action for recovery of the debt. It does not automatically reduce or extinguish the debt. Thus, in the above example, Jean would be entitled to sue John for £500. John would then be able to plead compensation of £200, so the court would only grant decree for £300.

(2) Unless both debts arise out of the same contract, or one of the parties is bankrupt, the debts must both be liquid, i.e. actually due and of an ascertained amount.

(3) There must be *concursus debiti et crediti* (concurrence of debt and credit). This concept has been explored in Chapter 9 in relation to retention. The parties must be debtor and creditor in the same capacity as well as at the same time.

PRESCRIPTION

Not all rights last forever, although some do, such as the right to recover stolen property. However, many rights do come to an end after a certain period of time, *i.e.* they "prescribe". Most obligations under contract prescribe after five years (short negative prescription) and this includes the right to payment. Certain other rights, *e.g.* relating to land, are subject to the long negative prescription of 20 years, but that is not of concern at this point. Also, certain rights may be acquired by positive prescription, but this has nothing to do with termination of contract.

It is essential that the period of time is unbroken. If the period is interrupted, the running of the period is not only stopped, it goes back to "zero" and starts running again. An interruption can take place by a "relevant claim" (creditor raises a court action or refers the matter to arbitration) or by "relevant acknowledgement" (debtor has shown signs of performing or has admitted in writing that the obligation still exists).

An example of this in practice would be where, after a debt has been unpaid for two years, the debtor writes to his creditor, acknowledging that the debt is still owing. This puts the running of the period back to zero, because it is a "relevant acknowledgement". The creditor now has a new period of five years to extract his debt.

Prescription is of ancient origin, but the modern law is found in the Prescription and Limitation (Scotland) Act 1973 as amended. In some cases a creditor may have personally barred himself (Chapter 2), *e.g.* by *mora* and taciturnity, from making a claim, although, in practice, such a plea is not common.

It is worth noticing one specialised but highly important point in relation to the law of leases of heritable property. Even though a lease is clearly for a fixed period of time, if neither landlord nor tenant gives notice of his wish to terminate, the lease runs on by operation of law through an automatic process known as "tacit relocation". Leases for one year or more will be extended by a year. Those for a lesser period will be extended for the same period as their existing duration.

IMPOSSIBILITY

A valid contract may be formed, but subsequent, or "supervening", events, outwith the power of both parties, make it impossible to perform. The courts do not expect parties to do what is impossible and damages for breach of contract will not be awarded. However, the obligation must be literally impossible to perform, not merely inconvenient or more expensive. In addition, the impossibility must not be due to the fault of the non-performing party. In *The Eugenia* (1964), it was known that part of a ship's voyage from Genoa to India, namely the Suez Canal, was a war zone, but the charterer ordered it to proceed by that route. The ship was detained in the canal, but the charterer could not escape damages. It was he who had been instrumental in causing the supervening event. The court conceded that performance was now impossible, but damages were still awarded.

A common example of impossibility is *rei interitus* (destruction of a thing) where the subject matter of the contract is destroyed. *Taylor v Caldwell* (1863): a music hall had been hired for a concert. After the hire had been agreed, the hall was badly damaged by fire. This was not due to the fault of the owner. The contract was terminated, without damages, on the grounds of impossibility.

Under section 7 of the Sale of Goods Act 1979, any contract for the sale of specific goods which perish, without fault of either party, before ownership passes from seller to buyer, is void.

There is a common law anomaly in a contract for the sale of heritable property in so far as the risk, as distinct from the ownership, passes to the buyer as soon as there is an agreement to buy. This rule applies even although the buyer has not taken entry, paid the price nor been given a legal title. In *Sloans Dairies Ltd v Glasgow Corporation* (1977), agreement had been reached for the sale of some tenement property. Before the price was paid, the building was destroyed by fire. The full purchase price still had to be paid. In practice, it is common, in contracts for the sale of heritable property, to provide that risk remains with the seller until the buyer takes entry. The Scottish Law Commission has recommended the statutory reversal of the common law rule (Report No.127, 1990).

Sometimes subjects are not literally destroyed but, to all intents and purposes, they might as well have been. This is known as "constructive" destruction and has the same effect as actual destruction, as in *London and Edinburgh Shipping Co. v The Admiralty* (1920), where a ship had been very badly damaged but had not actually sunk. In *Tay Salmon Fisheries v Speedie* (1929), a salmon fishing lease on part of the River Tay was terminated when the Government declared a stretch of the river an aerial bombing zone. Similarly, in *Mackeson v Boyd* (1942), the lease of a mansion house was terminated when the building was requisitioned by the military authorities.

It might also be impossible for a contract to be performed due to the condition of one of the parties. A common example would be breakdown of health, as in *Robinson v Davidson* (1871), where a pianist was unable to fulfil a contract to play. Similarly, in *Condor v Barron Knights* (1966), a drummer in a pop group had contracted to play at a very heavy schedule of appearances. The contract was terminated, as a result of a doctor's advice that his health would break if he attempted to adhere to the agreed schedule.

The fact that a contract has become more expensive or more difficult does not make it impossible to perform. *Davis Contractors v Fareham Urban District Council* (1956): a builder had agreed to construct 78 houses within eight months for a fixed sum. Due to shortages of labour and material, bad weather and inflation, the builder found himself substantially out of pocket. However, as performance was not impossible, the builder was not entitled to have the contract terminated. Most building contracts routinely allow for rises in costs due to materials, wages, or inflation.

If the impossibility is due to the substantial neglect or default of one of the parties, the possibility of damages would be open. However, the courts will not grant a decree *ad factum praestandum* where an obligation is impossible, whether or not there is fault.

ILLEGALITY

The rule here is quite simple. If a valid contract is formed but a subsequent change in the law, or political circumstances, such as outbreak of war, make performance illegal, the contract is at an end. Indeed, it may be a criminal offence to continue with performance. *Fraser & Co. Ltd v Denny, Mott & Dickson Ltd* (1944): a contract for the supply of pine timber was terminated. Although stocks were available, supply had become illegal, due to wartime restrictions. Naturally, if a contract is illegal when it is formed, it is void *ab initio* (from the beginning) and does not require to be terminated, although the court may have to adjudicate on the relative positions of the parties.

FRUSTRATION

Frustration, from the Latin *frustra* (in vain), can terminate a contract which is perfectly valid and, at least in theory, can be performed, but subsequent events, outwith the control of either party, have made the end result of performance materially different from what the parties originally had in mind. The concept of frustration can be well illustrated by two cases popularly known as the "coronation cases", because they arose from difficulties arising from the postponement of the coronation of Edward VII due to the king's illness. *Krell v Henry* (1903): a contract was formed for the hire of rooms in Pall Mall to overlook the coronation procession. In theory, it would have been possible for the contract to be performed, *i.e.* the hiring of the room, but the outcome—looking at the London traffic instead of the procession—would have been so radically different from what the parties originally had in mind as to frustrate the contract. By contrast, in *Herne Bay Steamboat v Hutton* (1903), there was a contract for the hire of a pleasure boat to watch the review of the fleet off Spithead by the king. Although the king was unable to attend, the fleet was still there and it was possible to enjoy the special outing; the contract was not frustrated. In *Jackson v Union Marine Insurance* (1874), a charterparty (hire of a ship) provided for a ship to proceed from Liverpool to Newport and pick up a cargo of iron for San Francisco. On its way to Newport, the ship grounded on a sandbank in Caernarfon Bay. It took several months to refloat her and carry out major repairs. Meanwhile, the charterer had put his goods on another ship. The original charterparty was held to have been frustrated. Whilst it would still have been possible for the original ship to proceed to San Francisco, the outcome would have been very different, due to the long delay.

By contrast, it should be noted that frustration, like impossibility, does not terminate a contract merely because performance has become more expensive. Where a ship bound for Britain had to take the longer route round the Cape of Good Hope due to the sudden closure of the Suez Canal in 1956, the charterparty was not frustrated (*Tsakiroglou & Co. Ltd v Noblee Thorl GmbH* (1962)).

Sometimes frustration is used in a wider sense, where it covers not only frustration as explained above, but also illegality and impossibility.

MONEY BACK?

In the case of frustration, impossibility or illegality, it is possible that money may have been paid in advance. This falls to be paid back, although, strictly speaking, not under the law of contract but under an action for repetition (repayment) known as the *condictio causa data causa non secuta* (action applicable when consideration has been given and consideration has not followed). In *Cantiere San Rocco SA v Clyde Shipbuilding and Engineering Co.* (1923), a Scottish company had agreed to supply engines to an Austrian company, payment to be by instalments. One instalment had been paid, but no engines were supplied as the outbreak of the First World War made performance illegal. After the war, the Austrian company was able to recover the deposit.

APPENDIX: SAMPLE EXAMINATION QUESTIONS AND ANSWER PLANS

1.   *With reference to the law of contract, the law of Scotland places great store on "the essentials" of a valid contract. What are these essentials?*

The only problem with a straightforward substantive question of this nature is that you have to answer it fairly fully. There is little opportunity for "on the one hand and on the other hand". Either you know the basic law or you do not. It is particularly important not to imagine that the examiner is going to read your mind. Assume that you are explaining the basic law to someone who is intelligent and quick on the "uptake" but has no previous knowledge of the subject. In that way, you should not go wrong.

The question covers the three essential elements of a contract:

Agreement about the same thing
You can cover the well tried paths of *consensus in idem*, citing such cases as *Raffles v Wichelhaus* (1864). Take care in applying cases. Two factors which tend to irritate examiners are: (1) students who, by rote, merely

repeat the facts of the case without showing its relevance and (2) students who merely "name-drop" by saying "see the case of" and leave it to the examiner to fill in the details. What if you remember a case but, in the heat of the moment, cannot remember the names of the parties? It is better to say "In the case of A against B" or "In a settled case" than to omit it altogether, just because you have forgotten the name. Remember, you are out to achieve every mark possible and examiners do look for you to give authority for what you say. At the same time, examiners are looking to see if they can pass you. They are not searching for ways to ensure that you fail. There is normally no need to remember the dates of cases, unless the context shows otherwise.

At least two contracting parties with capacity
This part of the question should not take long. The need for there being at least two contracting parties may be painfully obvious, but it should still be stated. A surprisingly large number of students forget to state the obvious in examination as though it were somehow beneath their dignity. Do not waste too much time going into the subject of capacity, but explain briefly what it is and give a couple of examples of where a party may lack capacity or have only partial capacity.

"Legal" obligations
There should be plenty of material here. Outline those agreements which are clearly illegal, due to immorality, criminality, public policy or statutory provision. There are other agreements which are perfectly legal but which the courts will not enforce, such as social agreements. Lastly, there is ample case law to show that the law will not traditionally enforce *sponsiones ludicrae* (sportive promises) such as gambling and wagering agreements.

2. (a) What is the distinction between a contractual offer and a willingness to negotiate? Why is the distinction important?

   (b) Joan is a hard-up student; she goes into a Summerways Supermarket and fills up a trolley with groceries. She wheels it to the checkout and states to the operator that she intends to buy the entire contents of the trolley for £10, although the market value is around £20. Comment on the legal issues involved.

   (c) George discusses the possible sale of his car to Mildred, although they are unable to come to an agreement. Somewhat frustrated, George writes to Mildred stating that he will sell the car for £3,000 and concludes the letter "If I do not hear from you by Friday, I shall treat the deal as concluded." Comment on the legal issues involved.

This question involves a small part of substantive law and then invites comment on two possible *scenarios*.

(a) Difference between offer and willingness to negotiate

This is a well tried but crucial area, namely formation of contract. An indication of willingness to negotiate is exactly what it says. Parties have not got beyond the preliminary stages and may still be thinking of making or receiving an offer. A familiar area is that of shops, which do not offer to sell items to the general public (*Pharmaceutical Society of Great Britain v Boots Cash Chemists* (1952)). An offer, on the other hand, is open for acceptance and once it is accepted without qualification, a binding contract is formed. A willingness to negotiate, by contrast, can never be accepted, because it is not an offer. Thus a shop cannot be forced to sell any item if it does not wish to. A further important point is that an offer must always come before an acceptance.

How is it possible to tell the difference? Every case has to be considered on its own merits. As well as goods in shops, advertisements, goods in catalogues and estimates are usually considered to be willingness to negotiate. Offers may be made expressly (verbally or in writing) or by implication. Good case on an unusual offer is *Chapleton v Barry UDC* (1940). Contrasting cases identifying mere willingness to negotiate and firm offer are *Harvey v Facey* (1893) and *Philp & Co. v Knoblauch* (1907) respectively.

A brief mention could also be made of offers to the general public (*Carlill v Carbolic Smokeball Co.* (1893), etc.) but be careful not to get side-tracked into a good story and let your pen run away with you!

(b) Problem number 1

An easy problem, but take time to explain it logically. The legal points at issue are the status of goods in shops (*i.e.* that they are a mere willingness to negotiate), who makes the offer and at what point in time. Using the facts from the *Boots* case, it is clear what the status of goods is. It is also clear that it is the customer who makes the offer when he takes the items to the point of sale. Accordingly, even although goods are price marked or bar-coded, any customer is entitled to make his own offer for any item or collection of items. Obviously, the checkout operator is unlikely to accept, in which case the customer's offer falls.

(c) Problem number 2

It is possible to have both an offer and acceptance by implication but the law generally takes a dim view of offers being unilaterally imposed on anyone. Sometimes an acceptance can be implied by a failure to reject, but this can only arise if there have been similar dealings between the parties in the past. As there is no evidence of similar dealings in the present case, there is no contract. You could also mention the statutory provisions of the Unsolicited Goods and Services Act 1971.

3.   *John has worked for six years for an employment agency which has offices in most of the cities and large towns in the United Kingdom. He has been offered a promoted post with another*

> *equally large agency and wishes to accept. His prudent employer*
> *points out that he cannot take up such a post within one year of*
> *leaving, due to a clause in his contract. This clause provides that*
> *he may not take up a post with any other employment agency "in*
> *order to prevent disclosure of the employers' system of work,*
> *presentation of the service to the customer and, in particular, the*
> *fee charging policy". Is this clause enforceable against John, in*
> *your reasoned opinion?*

This is the type of question which comes up in 101 different guises but basically asks the same thing and is popular with examiners.

It is important to be aware that there is not one obvious answer and that the problem needs to be addressed in such a way as to highlight the main legal issues. You should certainly come to your own conclusion based on your interpretation of these issues. A fair minded examiner—and the vast majority are very fair minded—should not penalise a candidate merely because a different conclusion from his own is drawn *provided* the candidate argues his case well. Indeed, an examiner will probably prefer a conclusion with which he disagrees to the totally open-ended conclusion "It could be this but on the other hand it could be that.". Of course there are two sides to any question but it is part of a lawyer's forensic training and skill to identify the strengths and weaknesses of both sides.

Identify the main area of law
What John is faced with is a restrictive covenant, which restricts a person's freedom to work where he pleases, for whom he pleases and in what line of business he pleases.

The general rule of law
As a very general rule, a restrictive covenant is only going to be upheld if it passes the test of being reasonable. It is reasonable to protect trade secrets and to prevent customers being enticed away. It is not reasonable to prevent fair competition.

The interpretation of what is reasonable
The courts tend to interpret "reasonable" rather more strictly where the contention is between employer and employee than they do as between the buyer and seller of a business—so this is already a point in John's favour.

Factors taken into account
As well as relying on the notoriously elusive concept of reasonableness, the court will take other factors into account, such as the type of the business, the radius or customer area it serves, where it is located, *e.g.* city, large town, small town or rural and the status of the employee. Make sure you cite cases. Established favourites are *Mason v Provident*

Clothing (1913), *Fitch v Dewes* (1921) and *Bluebell Apparel v Dickinson* (1980), but there are others quoted in the text. A great deal will depend on the status of John within the agency and we cannot assume what we are not told. If he occupies a fairly ordinary position, then that is in his favour. The agency appears to operate on a countrywide basis and it is clearly a blow that any employee will go to work for the arch-rival. The question is whether that move could reasonably threaten trade secrets or customer base. Trade secrets need not be of a purely industrial or manufacturing basis. The present writer would suggest that, in context, the clause is enforceable. Of course, only a court can ultimately decide. It is probably worth pointing out as a parting shot that the courts will only uphold or strike down clauses of this nature and will not alter them.

4. (a) *In which circumstances is a party entitled to treat a contract as having been breached?*
   (b) *Give a reasoned opinion of the remedy available to the aggrieved party in each of the following situations:*
      (1) *Cecil has been having a new bathroom suite installed by Loobylose Bathrooms. The centre of attraction was to have been the marble effect sunken bath with its gold-plated taps. The bathroom was satisfactorily completed apart from the bath—and it is now six weeks overdue.*
      (2) *Blue Marmalade, a famous pop group have signed up to give a concert at the Saturn Centre in Edinburgh. On the night of the concert, they fail to appear.*
      (3) *Sid, a self-employed taxi driver, has put his vehicle into a garage for servicing. The work has been done but Sid is experiencing cash-flow problems and cannot pay the bill. Sid is insisting that the garage return the vehicle as he needs it to earn the money to pay for the service.*

(a) Breach of contract
A party is in breach if he fails to perform the contract. This may be total non-performance, partial performance or defective performance. Unless a party fulfils his obligations in full, he is, at least technically, in breach. It may be important, in practice, to establish whether or not a breach can be treated as material, as the remedy of rescission is only available in such cases. At least in theory, any breach of contract can give rise to a claim for damages. The other point to be addressed is whether the breach has already taken place or whether it may take place in the future, *i.e.* anticipatory breach. If it is the latter, the innocent party has two choices: he may treat the contract as having been repudiated there and then and proceed accordingly in an action for damages (*White & Carter (Councils) Ltd v McGregor* (1962)); alternatively, he could presume that the contract is still alive and wait until the set time for performance. If the performance does take place, then clearly there has been no breach. If

performance does not take place, then clearly an action for damages may be raised. In this case, the damages may well be substantial.

(b)(1) Delay in performance
Delay is a common and problematic breach of contract. What the innocent party should do is probably as much a matter of pragmatism as of law. However, the crucial area in law is whether "time is of the essence" of a particular contract. If it is of the essence, Loobylose are in material breach which would open the possibility of Cecil rescinding. It is futile to rescind a contract when the innocent party wishes performance. It may at least be unwise to try to rescind a contract where *restitutio in integrum* is not possible. The delay in fitting the bath may be annoying but, unless the parties have agreed that time is of the essence, mere delay will, at best, only give rise to nominal damages (*Webster v Cramond Iron Co.* (1975)). You might argue that, by implication, time is of the essence of this contract. It would certainly be inconvenient, though not impossible, to live without a bath for such a long period of time. Even if you could muster an argument that time is of the essence, and that the contractor is in material breach, there is little point in rescinding the contract immediately, since *restitutio* cannot be given. However, prudent advice to Cecil might be to give Loobylose an ultimatum to the effect that work must be completed within a reasonable time. If it is not, Cecil will pay Loobylose for what work has been done on a *quantum meruit* basis and the bath will be supplied and fitted by other contractors. Cecil will seek damages from Loobylose for additional costs involved plus a sum to compensate for the inconvenience involved. It is just possible that Loobylose have a valid reason; war may have broken out with the country in which the supplier of this type of bath is manufactured! Whilst this is unlikely, it is important, in giving advice, to ensure that any party in breach has an opportunity to explain himself. This is no more than natural justice.

(b)(2) Total non-performance
This is a simple question and, you can answer it briefly, but not too briefly. It is as clear an example as you will find of breach by total non-performance. There is no point in advising the promoter to attempt specific implement. It is a waste of time to ask the court to grant a decree *ad factum praestandum* as the time of the concert is past. Performance is impossible and such a decree would not be awarded. Blue Marmalade have, by their non-appearance, repudiated the contract. The promoter can claim damages, which could well be substantial.

(b)(3) The defensive measure of lien
The garage is perfectly entitled to exercise a right of lien over the vehicle, pending payment of the bill. Sid has no right to insist that vehicle be returned, although common sense dictates that a taxi driver does not have much opportunity of earning money without a taxi at his disposal. If,

however, the garage agrees to return his taxi on the understanding that he will earn enough money to pay the bill, you would be duty bound to point out that they have now lost their right of lien. If Sid does not pay the bill, the garage cannot unilaterally repossess the taxi as a right of lien does not run with the goods (*Hostess Mobile Catering v Archibald Scott Ltd* (1981)).

5. (a) Give an account of the application and effect of impossibility, illegality and frustration on a contract.

 (b) A firm of builders undertake to build a number of flats for a Housing Association at a fixed price of £750,000. Due to shortage of building materials and skilled labour, to say nothing of inclement weather, the job takes many months longer than expected and costs the builder almost £1 million. Comment on the legal issues involved.

 (c) Muthill United F.C. sign up Oscar Deadeye, a very promising striker from another club. Not long after his joining the club, there is a terrible blizzard which leads to a power cut, causing the central heating in Oscar's house to fail. His goal-scoring foot, which is protruding from under the duvet, becomes frost-bitten and the striker has to have a toe amputated. Oscar's days as a striker are done. Discuss the legal issues involved.

(a) Impossibility, illegality and frustration

It is important to notice that if a contract is terminated by any of these three possibilities, damages are not payable. Obviously, anyone in breach of contract, will want to consider whether any one of these three "cards" could be played. If the reason for impossibility, illegality or frustration is the substantial fault of the party who is unable to perform, he cannot escape potential liability for damages. In addition, the cause for the inability to perform must be "supervening", *i.e.* it must have arisen since the contract was formed due to some external factor over which the parties have no control.

Impossibility means what is says: the contract must be impossible to perform, not merely inconvenient, expensive, or based on an error of judgement. An easy example of impossibility is *rei interitus*, where specific property essential to the contract is destroyed (*Taylor v Caldwell* (1863)) or constructively destroyed (*Mackeson v Boyd* (1942) or *Tay Salmon Fisheries v Speedie* (1929)). Depending on the number of marks allocated to this question, you could also make brief mention of the fact that there is a common law rule which provides that a buyer of heritable property assumes the risk as soon as missives are concluded (*Sloans Dairies Ltd v Glasgow Corporation* (1977)), unless expressly provided to the contrary. In the case of moveable property there is a statutory provision (Sale of Goods Act 1979, s.7) that where specific goods perish, without fault of either party, before ownership passes to the buyer, the contract is void. It might also be impossible to perform a contract due to the ill health of one of the parties, if *delectus personae* was a factor (*Condor v Barron Knights* (1966)).

Illegality, as a means of terminating a contract, occurs when the obligations were perfectly legal at the time of formation but supervening elements, beyond the control of the parties, have made performance illegal (*Fraser & Son v Denny, Mott & Dickson* (1944)). This is quite different from illegality at the outset. In the latter case, the contract would be void *ab initio*.

Frustration takes place where a contract can, at least in theory, be performed but because of supervening events outwith the control of the parties, performance produces a quite different outcome from what the parties had originally intended. It would be hard to resist citing the two contrasting Coronation cases of *Krell v Henry* (1903) and *Herne Bay Steamboat v Hutton* (1903).

(b) The builder's problem
Obviously this builder is learning a hard lesson. The fact that a contract has become difficult or expensive to perform does not make it impossible. A case very much in point is *Davis Contractors v Fareham UDC* (1956).

(c) The striker's problem
Even the most litigious lawyer would be hard pressed to blame a blizzard on any particular person (other than God?). It is agreed that there was a power cut. Is there any mileage in suing the electricity supply company? You could look at remoteness of damage—*Hadley v Baxendale* (1854) and related cases, including particularly *Balfour Beatty v Scottish Power* (1994). The conclusion would be "no". You could try to prove that Oscar had failed to take proper care of his precious foot by leaving it sticking outside the duvet. The contract could be terminated on account of impossibility of performance (as in *Condor v Barron Knights* (1966)), but the Club could try to claim damages from Oscar as he has contributed to his own injury. Whether they would succeed is another matter.

INDEX

95

TITLES IN THE
LAWBASICS SERIES

100 Cases That Every Scots Law Student Needs to Know
General Editor: Kenneth McK. Norrie
ISBN: 0414 014 626

Agency *Law*Basics
Aidan ODonnell
ISBN: 0414 012 305

Commercial *Law*Basics, 2nd Ed
Nicholas Grier
ISBN: 0414 015 371

Constitutional *Law*Basics, 2nd Ed
Jane Convery
ISBN: 0414 014 340

Contract *Law*Basics, 2nd Ed
Alasdair Gordon
ISBN: 0414 015 126

Criminal *Law*Basics
Clare Connelly
ISBN: 0414 012 313

Delict *Law*Basics
Gordon Cameron
ISBN: 0414 012 33X

E.C. *Law*Basics
Janet Paterson
ISBN: 0414 014 030

Evidence *Law*Basics
David Sheldon
ISBN: 0414 012 364

Family *Law*Basics
Elaine Sutherland
ISBN: 0414 012 321

Human Rights *Law*Basics
Alastair Brown
ISBN: 0414 013 980

Property *Law*Basics
Ken Swinton
ISBN: 0414 013 735

Scottish Legal System *Law*Basics, 2nd Ed
Robert S. Shiels
ISBN: 0414 015 517

Succession *Law*Basics
Alasdair Gordon
ISBN: 0414 013 107

Trusts *Law*Basics
Roderick Paisley
ISBN: 0414 013 301

The above titles are all available from your local bookstore.

For further information on titles published by
W. Green, The Scottish Law Publisher, you can visit our website at:

www.wgreen.co.uk